African Arguments

African Arguments is a series of short books about Africa today. Aimed at the growing number of students and general readers who want to know more about the continent, these books highlight many of the longer-term strategic as well as immediate political issues. They will get to the heart of why Africa is the way it is and how it is changing. The books are scholarly but engaged, substantive as well as topical.

Series editors

Titles already published

Alex de Waal, *AIDS and Power: Why There is No Political Crisis – Yet*

Raymond W. Copson, *The United States in Africa: Bush Policy and Beyond*

Chris Alden, *China in Africa*

Tom Porteous, *Britain in Africa*

Julie Flint and Alex de Waal, *Darfur: A New History of a Long War*, revised and updated edition

Jonathan Glennie, *The Trouble with Aid: Why Less Could Mean More for Africa*

Peter Uvin, *Life after Violence: A People's Story of Burundi*

Bronwen Manby, *Struggles for Citizenship in Africa*

Camilla Toulmin, *Climate Change in Africa*

Orla Ryan, *Chocolate Nations: Living and Dying for Chocolate in West Africa*

Theodore Trefon, *Congo Masquerade: The Political Culture of Aid Inefficiency and Reform Failure*

Forthcoming

Mary Harper, *Getting Somalia Wrong? Faith, War and Hope in a Shattered State*

Gerard McCann, *India and Africa – Old Friends, New Game*

Gernot Klantschnig and Neil Carrier, *Africa and the War on Drugs: Narcotics in Sub-Saharan Africa*

Tim Allen, *Trial Justice: The Lord's Resistance Army, Sudan and the International Criminal Court*, revised and updated edition

Published by Zed Books with the support of the following organizations:

International African Institute The International African Institute's principal aim is to promote scholarly understanding of Africa, notably its changing societies, cultures and languages. Founded in 1926 and based in London, it supports a range of seminars and publications including the journal *Africa*. <www.internationalafricaninstitute.org>

Royal African Society Now more than a hundred years old, the Royal African Society today is Britain's leading organization promoting Africa's cause. Through its journal, *African Affairs*, and by organizing meetings, discussions and other activities, the society strengthens links between Africa and Britain and encourages understanding of Africa and its relations with the rest of the world. <www.royalafrican society.org>

Social Science Research Council The Social Science Research Council brings much-needed expert knowledge to public issues. Founded in 1923 and based in New York, it brings together researchers, practitioners and policy-makers in every continent. <www.ssrc.org>

About the authors

Léonce Ndikumana is professor of economics at the University of Massachusetts, Amherst. He served as director of operational policies and director of research at the African Development Bank from 2008 to 2011, and Chief of Macroeconomic Analysis at the United Nations Economic Commission for Africa from 2006 to 2008. He is a graduate of the University of Burundi and received his doctorate from Washington University in St Louis, Missouri.

James K. Boyce is professor of economics at the University of Massachusetts, Amherst, where he directs the programme on development, peacebuilding and the environment at the Political Economy Research Institute. His previous books include *Investing in Peace: Aid and Conditionality after Civil Wars*; *The Philippines: The Political Economy of Growth and Impoverishment in the Marcos Era*; and *A Quiet Violence: View from a Bangladesh Village* (co-authored with Betsy Hartmann). He is a graduate of Yale University and received his doctorate from Oxford University.

LÉONCE NDIKUMANA AND
JAMES K. BOYCE

Africa's odious debts

how foreign loans and capital flight bled a continent

Zed Books
LONDON | NEW YORK

in association with

International African Institute
Royal African Society
Social Science Research Council

Africa's odious debts: how foreign loans and capital flight bled a continent was first published in association with the International African Institute, the Royal African Society and the Social Science Research Council in 2011 by Zed Books Ltd, 7 Cynthia Street, London N1 9JF, UK and Room 400, 175 Fifth Avenue, New York, NY 10010, USA

www.zedbooks.co.uk
www.internationalafricaninstitute.org
www.royalafricansociety.org
www.ssrc.org

Cover designed by Rogue Four Design
Set in OurType Arnhem and Futura Bold by Ewan Smith, London
Index: <ed.emery@thefreeuniversity.net>
Printed and bound in Great Britain by Mimeo Ltd, Huntingdon, Cambridgeshire, PE296XX.

A catalogue record for this book is available from the British Library
US CIP data are available from the Library of Congress

ISBN 978 1 84813 458 4 hb
ISBN 978 1 84813 459 1 pb

Contents

Figures and tables

Photographs

Abbreviations

AfDB	African Development Bank
AU	African Union
BNP	Banque Nationale de Paris
BoP	balance of payments
DRC	Democratic Republic of the Congo
GDF	Global Development Finance
GDP	gross domestic product
HIPC	heavily indebted poor country
HNWI	high net worth individual
IFAD	International Fund for Agricultural Development
IFI	international financial institution
IMF	International Monetary Fund
LIC	low-income country
MDG	Millennium Development Goal
OECD	Organisation for Economic Co-operation and Development
UNECA	United Nations Economic Commission on Africa
UNICEF	United Nations International Children's Emergency Fund

Acknowledgements

We incurred a number of debts in writing this book. Quite unlike the odious debts of our title, we are pleased to acknowledge them.

We thank Stephanie Kitchen of the International African Institute, Ken Barlow of Zed Books and Alex de Waal and Richard Dowden, the editors of the *African Arguments* series, for valuable advice and encouragement; Robert Molteno and Lawrence Lifschultz, who first suggested that we write this book; and Elizabeth Asiedu, Mwangi wa Githinji, Frank Holmquist, Isaac Kanyama, Roger King and Floribert Ngaruko for comments on earlier drafts. The usual caveats apply.

We thank Kaouther Abderrahim, Leila Davis, Grace Chang and James Garang for superb research assistance, and Judy Fogg of the Political Economy Research Institute at the University of Massachusetts, Amherst, among other things for her help in obtaining the photograph rights.

We also thank Hippolyte Fofack, who organized the Senior Policy Seminar on Capital Flight in Sub-Saharan Africa held in Pretoria in November 2007, as well as the seminar's participants for their insights and encouragement.

Last, but not least, we thank the many individuals in Africa and abroad who are striving to build a world free of injustice, impunity and financial chicanery.

Abuse is not sanctified by its duration or abundance; it must remain susceptible to question and challenge, no matter how long it takes.

– Chinua Achebe, *Home and Exile*, 2000

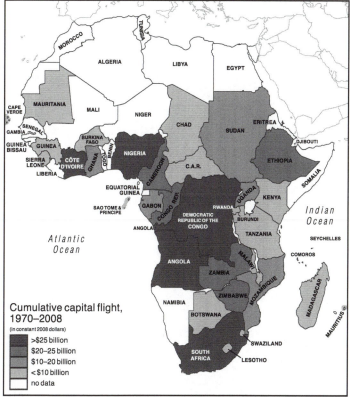

Cumulative capital flight,
1970–2008

(in constant 2008 dollars)

■ >$25 billion
■ $20–25 billion
■ $10–20 billion
■ <$10 billion
□ no data

Source: Authors' computations reported in Table A.2.

To our families

Introduction

As the Concorde lifted off the Gbadolite runway in June 1989, Joseph Mobutu had reasons to feel happy. Backed by generous international patronage, above all from the United States, he was one of the longest-serving heads of state in the world. His rule had brought impressive changes to Gbadolite, his home village in the far north of Zaire: his opulent palace, an airport big enough for the supersonic aircraft to come and go, an electric power plant to service them both. His rule had also brought great wealth to Mobutu himself. In a classified memo, the US State Department had estimated his fortune at $5 billion.[1] Mobutu publicly claimed a more conservative $50 million. Whatever the true number – most likely, somewhere in between – it was an impressive haul in a country where the average person lived on 60 cents a day.

In Washington, DC, where the Concorde was carrying him, Mobutu would meet his old friend George Bush, the new president of the United States. He would be the first African ruler to be received by Bush in the White House. The diplomatic grapevine reported that Bush's wayward son, George W., was starting to take an interest in politics. Maybe one of Mobutu's sons would take note and follow suit.

But Mobutu had reasons to feel just a little anxious, too. The Cold War was drawing to a close, and without it America might have less use for one of its 'oldest and most solid friendships in Africa', as President Reagan so graciously put it during Mobutu's 1986 visit to the White House.[2] To placate his tiresome critics in the US Congress – those whose goodwill could not be purchased with lavish hospitality in his Gbadolite palace, including wine flown in from Paris at a cost of $400 a bottle[3] – Mobutu was being pressed to ease political repression at home. This would entail risks. But the risks would be greater for his opponents,

1

should they mistake his forbearance for liberty, than for Mobutu himself.

Mobutu's more pressing worries were financial. Zaire's external debts now amounted to $9 billion. The country's creditors, alarmed by the dismal state of the economy and the disarray in public finances, were loath to lend more. Payments on past loans were overdue. If the International Monetary Fund (IMF), headquartered in Washington, could be persuaded to come to the rescue with a new loan, this would not only clear Zaire's IMF arrears but also provide the seal of approval that would convince other creditors to reschedule, too.

Getting a new IMF loan wouldn't be easy. A decade before, the Fund had installed its own staff members at the Bank of Zaire. The journal *Foreign Affairs* called this unusual step an effort to 'limit the hemorrhage of capital occurring both through the Zairian politico-commercial class as well as foreign mercantile groups', and predicted rightly that it would 'inevitably bring the group into conflict with the powerful political figures who are involved in capital flight'.[4] The results had not been happy. Erwin Blumenthal, the German central banker who led the IMF team, produced a scathing report that concluded that the 'impossibility of control over frauds' meant that there was 'not any – I repeat any – chance on the horizon that the numerous creditors of Zaire will recoup their funds'.[5]

In 1987, the IMF nevertheless approved a new loan to Zaire under pressure from the US government, over strong objections by senior staff and a rare dissenting vote by three members of the Fund's twenty-four-member executive board. This was among the decisions that prompted the resignation of David Finch, director of the IMF's exchange and trade relations department, who publicly decried 'the intrusion of political factors' into Fund lending and warned that 'balance-of-payments assistance in such conditions is indistinguishable from political support'.[6]

Last year, no less a personage than Michel Camdessus, the managing director of the IMF, told a newspaper that much of the debt problem of developing countries was due to corruption.

1 Zaire's president Joseph Mobutu was the first African head of state to be received by President George H. W. Bush in the White House, in June 1989 (George Bush Presidential Library and Museum)

'There are people there whose limitless egoism pushes them to deposit their money overseas,' he declared, 'which incurs a terrible flight of capital.' Mobutu denounced such criticism as 'scandalous', offering his own investments in Gbadolite as evidence that African leaders keep their money at home, not in foreign bank accounts.[7]

Despite these annoyances, Mobutu still had friends in high places. In addition to President Bush he could count on his long-time confidant, Jacques de Groote, now an executive director at the IMF and World Bank.[8] Earlier in the year Mobutu had enlisted the services of Washington lobbyist Edward van Kloberg III, paying him a retainer of $300,000 a year to secure favourable press coverage of Mobutu as a reliable US ally and to belittle his increasingly vocal American detractors as 'a cabal of left-wing extremists and homosexuals'.[9]

In the end, Mobutu's Washington visit was a resounding success. At the White House, President Bush lauded him as 'one of our most valued friends' on the entire continent of Africa, and announced that Zaire had taken 'the constructive step of signing an economic policy reform agreement with the International Monetary Fund'.[10] The IMF came through with $187 million in fresh lending. The World Bank chipped in $87 million more, lifting Zaire's cumulative debt to the Bank to more than $900 million.

§

While Mobutu was once again shaking the money tree in Washington, one of this book's authors, Léonce Ndikumana, a junior university lecturer in Burundi, Zaire's neighbour, was witnessing historic changes in his country. The 'wind from the West' was invigorating long-standing popular demands for democratic opening in Burundi and across Africa. In September 1988, Léonce joined twenty-six Burundian intellectuals in signing an open letter to President Pierre Buyoya, urging the government to stop army killings of civilians in the northern communes of Ntega and Marangara, and to begin a transition to democratic rule. This seemingly simple exercise in democracy was deemed an offence to the nation, and it earned Léonce and six other signatories

4

five months of solitary confinement in the notorious maximum-security prison of Mpimba.

The open letter, which cited well-documented facts about indiscriminate killings in the north of the country and suggested positive ways to find solutions to ethnic conflict by addressing its root causes, threw the government off balance. It attracted attention in the resident diplomatic community and internationally, being seen as an opportunity to launch a national debate to initiate a transition towards an open and inclusive political system. The government came under pressure to release the jailed *signataires*. In the books of international human rights organizations, such as Amnesty International, Léonce joined the ranks of those referred to as 'prisoners of conscience'. This attention helped to secure his release from prison in February 1989.

Léonce emerged from prison with an enhanced thirst to better understand the relationships between development and politics in African countries. He wished to better understand the role of the Western powers in Africa's economy and politics. Above all, he wanted to understand why the people of countries like neighbouring Zaire, a darling of the Western aid donors, could remain so poor while their country was so rich.

Upon his release, Léonce was appointed Chief Finance Officer and then Director of Finance and Administration at the University of Burundi. He won a fellowship from the US Agency for International Development to pursue doctoral studies in economics at Washington University in St Louis in the United States. This was an opportunity to pursue his quest for greater understanding of African development challenges. He seized it, and left Burundi in August 1990.

§

At the time of Mobutu's rewarding trip to Washington, DC, the second author of this book, James Boyce, was writing a book on the development strategy that had been pursued in the Philippines under Ferdinand Marcos. Like Mobutu, Marcos was an authoritarian ruler backed for many years by the United States – until his overthrow by the 'People's Power' revolution

5

of February 1986. His regime, like Mobutu's, ran up enormous debts to foreign creditors.

When Marcos was airlifted into his Hawaiian exile aboard a US Air Force jet, he left behind a Philippine external debt of more than $28 billion. This foreign borrowing ostensibly had been undertaken to advance the country's economic development, but in practice it had done little to improve the well-being of ordinary Filipinos. Average incomes remained virtually stagnant during his two-decade rule, and many of the poorest Filipinos saw their real incomes decline.[11] Meanwhile, Marcos and his cronies accumulated fortunes. Millions of dollars in looted funds were eventually traced to bank accounts in Switzerland and other havens, but the best indicator of the scale of the looting came in 1988 when Marcos, his health deteriorating, reportedly offered $5 billion to the new government to be allowed to return to the Philippines to die.[12] His offer was refused.

Not all of the money borrowed by the Marcos regime was siphoned into foreign bank accounts. The biggest single item in the Philippine debt, for instance, was a nuclear power plant built at a cost of more than $2 billion, including interest, a price that the Marcos government's own Secretary of Industry characterized as 'one reactor for the price of two'.[13] Loans to finance the reactor came from the US Export-Import Bank and from a private bank syndicate led by Citibank and American Express.[14] The price tag was inflated by multimillion-dollar kickbacks – more politely termed 'commissions' – paid to Marcos associates on contracts to build the reactor. In the end the nuclear plant never produced a kilowatt of electricity, among other reasons because it turned out to have been built in a seismic zone with a high earthquake risk. From the standpoint of the national economy, the project was a colossal waste of borrowed money. But from the standpoint of those who pocketed the kickbacks, the project was a brilliant success. The useless nuclear power plant was simply a social transaction cost of pursuing their personal objective: the transformation of public debts into private assets.

In an effort to better understand the linkages between foreign loans and capital flight in the Philippines, Boyce used statistical methods that had recently been developed by researchers at the World Bank and elsewhere to estimate the total amount of capital flight from the Philippines in the Marcos era. He arrived at a staggering result: $13 billion (in 1986 dollars); more than $19 billion if imputed interest earnings on flight capital were included in the total. By the latter measure, capital flight was equivalent to roughly two-thirds of the country's total foreign debt.

Investigating the relationship further, Boyce analysed the correlations between year-to-year variations in capital flight and year-to-year variations in foreign borrowing. He found that one dollar of additional foreign borrowing was associated with 54 cents of additional capital flight in the same year. He concluded that a 'revolving door' linked debt to capital flight in the Philippines, and that a substantial fraction of borrowed funds had quickly exited the country.

Boyce presented his findings in a monograph published in 1990 by the Philippine Institute of Development Studies, an agency of the country's planning ministry.[15] The study helped to fuel debate in the Philippines over how to deal with the foreign debt legacy of the Marcos era. The Freedom from Debt Coalition, a Philippine civil society organization, argued that debts arising from loans that had been diverted to illegitimate uses ought to be repudiated. Some senior government officials, including the country's planning minister, agreed. Others, including the central bank governor, maintained that the government should seek to remain in the good graces of international creditors by servicing all the inherited debts.[16] Boyce cited precedents in international law for the repudiation of 'odious debts', and suggested that if the government adopted such a strategy it could greatly ease its debt burden. But the Philippine government opted instead for the strategy of dutiful debt service, spending vast sums in the ensuing years to service foreign debts incurred in the Marcos era.

§

The collaboration that produced this book began in the mid-1990s at the University of Massachusetts, Amherst, where both

7

of the authors were teaching. Ndikumana, having completed his doctorate in economics at Washington University, had joined the UMass faculty; Boyce was chairing the economics department.

In Zaire, the Mobutu regime was coming to its bitter end. Mobutu's relationships with his external backers had deteriorated after his 1989 visit to Washington. Calling for an end to US assistance to the regime in March 1991, US Congressman Stephen Solarz, a member of the House subcommittee on Africa, declared that Mobutu 'has established a kleptocracy to end all kleptocracies, and has set a new standard by which all future international thieves will have to be measured'.[17] US development assistance, apart from food aid, was terminated in June 1991.[18] The IMF issued an official declaration of non-cooperation in February 1992, making Zaire ineligible for further borrowing, and suspended the country's voting rights in 1994.[19] At home, the war to succeed Mobutu and to seize control of the country's rich mineral resources was under way.[20] Over the next decade it would claim as many as five million lives – more than any other conflict since the Second World War.[21]

Mobutu fled his homeland in May 1997, as rebel forces closed in on the capital, Kinshasa. Four months later he died in exile in Morocco. The country he left behind was in economic ruin, political turmoil, and facing a massive humanitarian crisis. He also left behind a foreign debt that by that time, counting interest arrears, had swollen to $14 billion.

As the regime unravelled, we began to investigate the relationship between Zaire's debt and the capital flight the country had experienced under Mobutu's rule. In an article titled 'Congo's odious debt', published in the journal *Development and Change* in 1998, we estimated that capital flight from Zaire during the Mobutu regime amounted to $12 billion, a sum nearly equivalent to the total external debt passed to the successor government of the Democratic Republic of the Congo (DRC), as the country was renamed after Mobutu's overthrow. In the article, we provided documentary evidence that the creditors knew, or should have been aware, that a large fraction of their loans had gone into

8

the pockets of Mobutu and his coterie rather than benefiting the Congolese people.

Expanding our investigation of capital flight to other sub-Saharan African countries, we then wrote a second piece, 'Is Africa a net creditor?', which appeared in the *Journal of Development Studies* in 2001. We found that capital flight from twenty-five low-income African countries over the 1970–96 period amounted to $193 billion (and to $285 billion including imputed interest earnings). Comparing this to the $178 billion external debt of the same set of countries, we concluded that Africa was a net creditor to the rest of the world: the external assets of these countries exceeded their external debts. The key difference between the two, of course, is that the assets are in the hands of private individuals, whereas the debts are public, a liability of the African people through their governments. We were gratified when this article won the Dudley Seers Memorial Prize, named after the distinguished British economist.

In a third piece, 'Public debts and private assets', published in *World Development* in 2003, we extended our estimates to thirty African countries and statistically analysed the relationship between outflows of capital and inflows of external borrowing. We found that for every dollar of loan inflows, as much as 80 cents flowed back out as capital flight in the same year. These findings suggested that, to a substantial extent, African capital flight has been debt fuelled.

Some of the policy implications of our findings were spelled out in 'Africa's debt: who owes whom?', published in 2005 in a book edited by Gerald Epstein, *Capital Flight and Capital Controls in Developing Countries*. There we made the case that African countries have compelling ethical, economic and legal grounds for invoking the doctrine of odious debt and repudiating liabilities that cannot be demonstrated to have benefited the populace.

In 2007, we made a keynote presentation at the Senior Policy Seminar on Capital Flight from Sub-Saharan Africa organized by the Association of African Central Bank Governors, the Reserve Bank of South Africa, and the World Bank, in Pretoria, South

9

Africa. In this presentation we extended our quantitative analysis up to the year 2004, and discussed the case for selective repudiation of debts that financed capital flight – a policy proposal that has now moved from the 'radical fringe' to gain a hearing in the corridors of power both in Africa and in the international financial institutions.[22] Papers based on our presentation subsequently appeared in the *International Review of Applied Economics* and the *African Development Review*.[23]

§

Drawing upon more than a decade of research, this book updates our analysis of the relationship between foreign loans and capital flight. We have tried to present our findings in language that is accessible to lay readers. Readers interested in more technical treatments can refer to the scholarly publications mentioned above and listed in the bibliography.

Our analysis is based on the experience of sub-Saharan Africa during the last four decades, but the issues we address in this book are not exclusive to Africa. The parallels between the Philippines under Marcos and Zaire under Mobutu already have been suggested above. The revolving door linking foreign loans to capital flight has spun widely throughout the developing world. Writing on Latin America, economist Manuel Pastor described cases where 'an investor could draw a publicly-guaranteed external loan cheaply, and ship his/her own resources abroad to acquire foreign assets'.[24] James Henry, the former chief economist for the international consulting firm McKinsey & Company, observed that in some cases borrowed funds were deposited directly into private accounts in the same foreign banks that initiated the loan: 'the entire cycle is completed with a few bookkeeping entries in New York'.[25]

In Chapter 1, we provide examples that illustrate the role of foreign banks both as lenders of funds diverted abroad and as safe havens for flight capital. We examine the parallel between foreign loans in Africa and the 'liar loans' in US mortgage markets that precipitated the 2008 financial meltdown. And we document the magnitude of the negative net transfers that occur when debt service payments by African countries surpass the inflow of new money from fresh loans.

Chapter 2 traces the statistical detective work that is required to measure capital flight, and presents evidence that Africa is a net creditor to the rest of the world in that its external assets exceed its external debts. The assets are private, while the debts are public. Wealthy individuals hold the assets. The African people as a whole hold the debts through their governments.

Chapter 3 examines linkages between foreign loans and capital flight, and presents quantitative evidence that much of Africa's capital flight has been debt fuelled; that is, loans from foreign creditors to African governments wound up as private assets held abroad by individual Africans.

In Chapter 4, we document some of the human cost of this phenomenon, analysing the impact of debt service payments on public health expenditures and thereby on health outcomes such as infant mortality.

In Chapter 5 we conclude by discussing what can be done. We make the case for new policies and institutions, building upon the legal doctrine of odious debt, that would lift the current burden of servicing debts from which the public derived no benefit, and would change incentive structures in the international financial architecture so as to promote responsible behaviour by lenders and borrowers in the future.

We seek to demonstrate in this book that the diversion of foreign borrowing into capital flight is not simply a matter of misdeeds by a few corrupt officials, abetted by a few complacent or complicit bankers. Rather it is the product of systemic flaws in the international financial arrangements that govern borrowing and lending. The problem cannot be cured simply by identifying bad actors and weeding them out. The solution will require fundamental reforms that change the framework of incentives and opportunities in global finance.

1 | Tales from the shadows of international finance

In the simplified world of introductory economics textbooks, credit markets provide a valuable and straightforward service: they move money from savings into investments. The savers lend their money and are rewarded with interest. The investors borrow money on the expectation that the returns to their investment will cover the cost of interest payments. Banks connect the supply and demand sides of the credit market, and for this service, known as financial intermediation, they earn remuneration in two forms: fees, and the spread between the interest rates they pay on deposits and receive on loans.

In this textbook world, all is what it seems. Borrowers act in good faith, taking loans only when their expected benefits exceed expected costs. Bankers exercise due diligence, issuing loans only when they expect the borrower to repay. And no one would lend hundreds of millions of dollars to the Mobutu regime in 1989.

In the real world, matters are not so simple. Mobutu was a particularly flamboyant exemplar of a much broader class of individuals who have spun debts contracted in the name of the state into personal wealth, much of it stashed abroad. These individuals are aided and abetted by bankers who are willing and eager to make loans to governments with few questions asked, while at the same time courting deposits from 'high net worth individuals' who skim the borrowed funds into private accounts.

In the shadows of international finance, large sums of money routinely slip across borders, beneath the surface of officially recorded transactions and outside the box of the standard economics textbooks toolkit. To understand the realities of African development and underdevelopment, we must peer into these shadows.

Masters of disasters

When compelled to acknowledge the diversion of public loans into private pockets, international creditors sometimes seek solace in the thought that at least a fraction of their loans was used legitimately. 'If you take the amount of 30 percent loss,' a senior World Bank official told political scientist Jeffrey Winters, 'it means 70 cents [on the dollar] got used for development after all. That's a lot better than some places with only 10 cents on the dollar.' In testimony before the US Senate Committee on Foreign Relations in 2004, Winters explained that 'places with only 10 cents on the dollar' was a reference to 'certain Bank clients in Africa where nearly all of the loan funds are misallocated, diverted, unaccounted for, or simply stolen'.[1]

If these loans vanished without a trace, they would simply bypass the vast majority of Africans, with no impact on their well-being. From their perspective the loss would merely be what economists call an 'opportunity cost', forgone development that could otherwise have been financed with the missing money.

But the costs to the people of Africa go well beyond missed opportunities. The use of foreign loans for illegitimate private gains distorts both the politics and the economies of African countries. It bolsters the power of corrupt elites, and in so doing enhances their ability to manipulate government policies to advance their interests above those of their countrymen. And because these are loans, not grants or outright gifts, they leave behind a legacy of debt-service obligations that often persist long after the individuals who profited from the deals have departed from the scene.

The outcome is disastrous for African development. But it is lucrative for individual players on both sides of the credit market. As a result, private incentives are not aligned with the public good. A few examples will illustrate how this disjuncture has revealed itself in Africa.

Nigeria: the price of soft financial management The decade from 1984 to 1994 saw 'the most rampant corruption and governmental dysfunction in Nigeria's history', in the words of Steve Berkman,

13

former lead investigator in the World Bank's anti-corruption and fraud investigation unit. The World Bank ought to know: it loaned Nigeria $4.6 billion during this period.[2]

One of the recipients of World Bank loans was Nigeria's National Electric Power Authority (NEPA), the government agency responsible for generating and delivering electricity throughout the country. NEPA nominally had 4,700 megawatts of power-generating capacity by 1989, but its peak load was less than half that amount at 1,900 megawatts. Even that load could not be delivered on a reliable basis, forcing many firms and households to invest in their own backyard generators. Nigerians joked that NEPA stood for 'No Electric Power Anytime' (its successor, the Power Holding Company of Nigeria, or PHCN, was quickly re-branded 'Problem Has Changed Name'). Berkman explains why NEPA nevertheless chose to expand further its generating capacity:

> A new power-generating station can cost hundreds of millions of dollars, and that translates into large kickbacks for those in government who can facilitate contract awards and smaller kickbacks for those involved in supervising the civil works and procuring supplies and equipment. It can also result in lucrative subcontracts for shell companies owned by government officials, their relatives, and close associates – subcontracts in which payments are received for services not rendered or for material and equipment supplied at grossly inflated prices.[3]

In addition to bid-rigging and kickbacks, Berkman describes other practices that were commonplace in Nigeria: the procurement of unnecessary goods and services 'for the sole purpose of facilitating these activities'; the parking of funds in accounts from which interest earnings were then siphoned; and the creation of 'phony documents to cover up the diversion of funds from government accounts to private accounts'.[4] Procedural safeguards for disbursement of World Bank project loans could be 'easily breached', Berkman reports, 'through the submission of fraudulent documents to support the withdrawal applications'.

In the case of 'structural adjustment loans', which were not tied to specific projects but rather served as carrots for implementation of economic policy reforms prescribed by the Bank, there were even fewer controls on where the money went. Berkman wryly characterizes such loans as 'an excellent device to move a lot of money with a minimum of effort and without any accountability afterward'.[5]

These problems persisted under General Sani Abacha, who ruled Nigeria from 1993 to 1998. Abacha accumulated personal wealth estimated by the World Bank at $2 billion to $5 billion.[6] Nigerian president Olusegun Obasanjo would subsequently charge that Abacha 'siphoned $2.3 billion from the Treasury, awarded contracts worth $1 billion to front companies, and took $1 billion in bribes from foreign contractors'.[7]

A 2007 World Bank review of public expenditure management in Nigeria finds that financial reporting and monitoring remain a 'very weak area', leaving the government 'open to diversion of funds and outright corruption'. The review concludes that this state of affairs is not accidental, but instead is the result of deliberate decisions: 'These deficiencies are not technical so much as environmental, insofar as for many years "soft" financial management has been part of how the Federal Government has wanted to run its affairs.'[8]

Soft financial management afflicted Nigeria's use of both foreign loans and oil revenues. 'Nigeria owes $34 billion, much of it in penalties and compound interest imposed on debts that were not paid by the military dictatorships of the 1980s and early 1990s,' finance minister Ngozi Okonjo-Iweala observed in January 2005. 'We make annual debt repayments of more than $1.7 billion, three times our education budget and nine times our health budget.' Terming this situation 'unsustainable', Okonjo-Iweala called for debt cancellation.[9] Two months later, the Nigerian House of Representatives passed a resolution calling for a halt to external debt-service payments on the grounds that the country's economy had been 'devastated by a series of military regimes from 1984 to 1999 who stole billions of dollars from state coffers'.[10]

In October 2005, spurred by the outcry in Nigeria, the Paris

Club of creditor countries agreed to write off $18 billion of the $30 billion debt owed by the government to official lenders, led by the governments of Britain, France, Germany and Japan. As part of the deal, the government agreed to repay the other $12 billion, or roughly 40 cents on the dollar. Since the debt by that time included $4 billion in interest arrears, this was equivalent to 46 cents per dollar on the original loan amounts. If it is true that 'only 10 cents on the dollar' went into bona fide development, the Nigerian people did not get an enviable bargain.

In January 2006, eighteen US Congressmen called on the US Export-Import Bank and the US Agency for International Development to waive repayment of the $400 million they were still owed under the Paris Club deal. 'Much of Nigeria's debt can be considered odious,' they wrote to the US Treasury Secretary, 'given the fact that the original loans were made to authoritarian regimes – many of which were then looted while interest and penalties accumulated.'[11] Nigerian critics expressed similar reservations about the deal. But buoyed by high oil prices, the Nigerian government paid the final instalment of the $12 billion in April 2006, thereby completing the largest single transfer of wealth to foreign creditors in African history.

● *Congo-Brazzaville: oil-backed loans* Some African petroleum-exporting countries and creditors have forged an even tighter nexus between foreign loans, capital flight and oil. In 1979 the Republic of Congo (Congo-Brazzaville) took its first 'oil-backed loan' – a loan collateralized by a lien on future oil exports. The creditor was Elf, the French oil company. In the years that followed, oil-backed loans, often carrying much higher-than-average interest rates, became popular among private creditors, oil companies and African rulers.

To circumvent IMF strictures against this irregular borrowing, as well as to facilitate transfers into private accounts, oil-backed loans are often concealed by routing them through offshore entities. French researcher Maud Pedriel-Vassière describes the modus operandi:

16

The scheme is substantially the same in every case. First, one or several offshore companies receives a loan at preferential interest rates from a bank or buyer of crude oil. Then, these offshore companies lend to the sovereign state at significantly higher rates. The difference between the interest rates is ultimately collected by the original creditor, while the representatives of the regime and their close associates receive a juicy commission, as do various other middlemen.[12]

Banks that have provided oil-backed loans to the Republic of Congo include Crédit Agricole, Crédit Lyonnais and Banque Paribas.[13] The exorbitant interest rates on oil-backed loans in effect mean that creditors are able to obtain crude oil at a cost considerably below the world market price. In 1993, desperate for cash to pay state salaries as its oil exports were going to service its earlier oil-backed loans, Congo's government took a fresh $150 million loan from the US-based firm Occidental Petroleum, to be repaid with 50 million barrels of oil: a price of $3 per barrel at a time when the world market price was $17 per barrel.[14]

Political instability, exacerbated by the government's chronic fiscal crisis, soon spiralled into a civil war that claimed thousands of lives. Arms for both sides were financed through oil-backed loans. 'Rather than contributing to the welfare of the Congolese population,' an unpublished 2001 IMF report observed, 'the proceeds from oil-collateralized borrowing may have been used to finance combat operations during the civil war.'[15] In the words of the former head of Elf, 'Thousands of Congolese died, and now the survivors must pay for the arms that killed their loved ones.'[16]

Very little of Congo-Brazzaville's oil revenue – which accounts for 70 per cent of national income – has trickled down to the country's ordinary citizens. But the ruling elite has enjoyed a lavish lifestyle. Global Witness, the London-based organization that investigates abuses in the exploitation of natural resources, has documented the European shopping sprees of Denis Christel Sassou Nguesso, the son of Congo's president and head of the state agency that sells the country's oil. He spent thousands of

17

dollars per month at shops like the Parisian fashion house Louis Vuitton, billing his expenses to offshore companies that 'appear to have received, with other shell companies, money related to Congo's oil sales'.[17]

Mr Sassou Nguesso's shopping tabs became public information as a result of litigation by creditors known as 'vulture funds', which specialize in buying 'distressed debt' on secondary markets at a steep discount from its face value. These creditors, which are often hedge funds, then pursue legal actions in an effort to recover the face value, or something closer to it, with the aim of netting a handsome profit.[18] In this case, the creditors were seeking to prove that the government was concealing oil revenues that instead could have been used to repay the debts. Since 1990 private creditors have extracted more than $500 million in settlements and court judgments from the Republic of Congo.[19]

As of 2008, Congo-Brazzaville's external debt stood at almost $5.5 billion. In a nation of 3.6 million people, this amounted to more than $1,500 per person. That same year, according to World Bank data, 74 per cent of the country's population lived on less than $2 per day.[20]

Gabon: The Bongo system In Libreville, the capital of Gabon, elegant glass and marble palaces line Omar Bongo Triumphal Boulevard. These edifices were constructed at a cost of $500 million by President Omar Bongo, who ruled the country for four decades until his death in a Barcelona hospital in 2009.[21] A few months afterwards a *New York Times* reporter visiting Libreville described the grim scene behind the palaces – 'shacks and shanties stretching to the horizon, dirt roads and street vendors eking out a living selling cigarettes and imported vegetables'. The extreme juxtaposition of wealth and poverty in Gabon is a legacy of what its people call the 'Bongo system', succinctly defined by the *Times* as 'forsaking roads, schools and hospitals for the sake of Mr. Bongo's 66 bank accounts, 183 cars, 39 luxury properties in France and grandiose government constructions in Libreville'.[22]

In response to a legal complaint filed by three non-governmental

2 Republic of Congo's President Denis Sassou Nguesso welcomed French President Nicolas Sarkozy to Brazzaville in 2009 (Associated Press)

organizations, in 2007 the French police identified multiple bank accounts held by Bongo at BNP Paribas and Crédit Lyonnais. The police enquiries also revealed that Bongo's wife had purchased a luxury automobile at a cost of 326,000 euros (nearly half a million dollars), drawing the funds directly from the Gabonese treasury.[23]

Eight years earlier, in 1999, the US Senate Permanent Sub-committee on Investigations revealed that Bongo also held multiple personal accounts in the international private banking unit of New York-based Citibank. More than $130 million had passed through these accounts – located in the Channel Islands, New York, London, Paris, Luxembourg and Switzerland – in the preceding fifteen years.[24] Citibank responded to these revelations by closing the Bongo accounts, explaining to the Subcommittee on Investigations that it did so 'because of the cost of answering questions about them, rather than because of specific concerns about the source of funds or the reputational risk'.[25]

During Bongo's rule, Gabon – or more accurately, the country's political elite – received billions of dollars in revenues from oil exports. Remarkably little of this windfall was invested in the country's development. Today Gabon has more kilometres of oil pipelines than it does of paved roads.[26]

Gabon's oil revenues were supplemented by foreign loans, notably in the late 1970s and 1980s when the 650-kilometre trans-Gabon railway was constructed at a final cost of roughly $4 billion.[27] The World Bank refused to lend money to build the railway on the grounds that the project was economically unviable. Declaring that 'even if we have to deal with the devil, we will deal with the devil', Bongo turned instead to commercial creditors, who were happy to lend the money at market rates.[28] Together with the Inga-Shaba hydroelectric project in Mobutu's Zaire, the trans-Gabon railway became one of Africa's most famous white elephants – costly schemes 'stimulated by desire for political prestige and ready access to foreign financing', in the words of a former US aid official, resulting in 'massive external debt for little development impact'.[29]

White elephant projects have attractions apart from vanity:

3 French president Valéry Giscard d'Estaing received Gabon's president Omar Bongo in Paris in November 1977 (Agence France Press)

they create opportunities for some serious graft. Gabon's budget allocations for transportation and other public services were impressive. 'But in reality, it was actually about 20 per cent of what was on paper,' an aid official confided to the *New York Times*. 'The rest was embezzled.'[30]

The commercial banks that provided loans to Gabon's government included Banque Nationale de Paris (BNP), Crédit Lyonnais and Citibank – banks in which Bongo himself held personal accounts.[31] BNP chaired the steering committee of Gabon's 'London Club' of commercial bank creditors, and Citibank served as the group's agent bank.[32]

Citibank loans to Gabon helped to finance the purchase of equipment for the trans-Gabon railway as well as the purchase of aircraft for the national airline.[33] At the time of the US Senate hearings in 1999, the chief compliance officer for Citibank Private Bank stated, 'The Private Bank never has had a strategy to link efforts to get or retain a head of state's personal business in order to develop other business in that country.'[34] He neglected to mention whether there was any link in the reverse direction, whereby lending to a government opened the door to private banking for the same government's senior officials.

As of 2008, Gabon's external debt stood at almost $2.4 billion. In a nation with a population of 1.4 million, this amounted to more than $1,600 per person. According to the World Health Organization, 77 Gabonese children per 1,000 die before reaching their fifth birthday – triple the rate in Botswana, a country with roughly the same per capita national income.[35]

Subprime Africa

Why did creditors make billions of dollars in loans to regimes whose leaders put their personal economic interests ahead of their countries' economic development? Why did they fail to exercise due diligence by seeking to ensure that their loans were used for bona fide purposes, invested in projects whose returns would enable borrowing countries to pay them back with interest?

If the answer were simply incompetence on the part of some

lenders who were duped by irresponsible borrowers, we would expect to see differential outcomes, not systemic failures. Creditors who made unsound loans would lose their money, and either learn their lessons or exit the business. Over time, the invisible hand of the market would relentlessly weed out incompetence, and productive loans would be the rule rather than the exception.

The fact that Africa's public debts piled up, year after year, even as capital flight drained African economies and made timely and full repayment of these debts an impossibility, tells us that the problem was not simply creditor ignorance or ineptitude. These were transactions among consenting adults. The creditors were not naive babes in the woods. They included sophisticated international financial institutions (IFIs), such as the World Bank and the International Monetary Fund, the world's most powerful governments, and the world's biggest commercial banks. The creditors knew, or should have known, the score. And they continued to lend.

To understand why, we need to look into the structure of incentives on the lender side of credit markets. In both official institutions and private banks, these incentives elevated short-term lending targets above long-term repayment prospects. The result was a phenomenon known as 'loan pushing'.[36] What counted was the quantity of loans, not their quality.

Within the official lending institutions – the IFIs and the bilateral aid agencies and export credit agencies – there were (and still are) powerful incentives for loan officers to move the money. In part this stems from the use-it-or-lose-it syndrome in government agencies that are subject to annual budget cycles: failure to use appropriated funds by the end of the fiscal year may trigger reduced appropriations the following year. But even at the IFIs, which are to some extent insulated from the vagaries of legislative calendars, individual staff members know that their performance will be judged above all by their success in making loans. A loan officer who delays loans, or withholds them altogether from a willing borrower owing to concerns about leakage of the money into private pockets, is not on the fast track to a promotion. On the contrary, such recalcitrance is certain to annoy borrower governments, and their complaints may reach the ears of one's superiors.

In 1992, an internal evaluation by the World Bank's Portfolio Management Task Force (known as the 'Wapenhans report' after its leader) found that 37.5 per cent of Bank projects completed in 1991 could be categorized as failures, up from 15 per cent a decade before. Wapenhans concluded that the presence of an 'approval culture' at the Bank contributed to this trend.[37]

Observing that subsequent evaluations at the African Development Bank, Asian Development Bank and Inter-American Development Bank had all reached similar conclusions, the 1998 World Bank study *Assessing Aid* frankly summed up the situation: 'Securing loan approvals was a more powerful motivator for staff than working to ensure project success or larger development goals.'[38] Disbursements of funds are 'easily calculated and tended to become a critical output measure', the study's authors explained. 'Agencies saw themselves as being primarily in the business of dishing out money, so it is not surprising that much went into poorly managed economies – with little result.'[39]

A further motive for lending by official creditors – a motive that again is independent of the loan's productive impact in the borrowing country – is export promotion. In the case of export credit agencies (ECAs) such as the US Export-Import Bank, this is, in fact, the explicit primary objective. But it has also been a significant motive in bilateral official development assistance, the importance of which is reflected in correlations between the aid disbursements and donor exports.[40] Multilateral creditors are also aware of the political salience of export contracts: the World Bank, for example, maintains state-level procurement records in the USA 'in order to facilitate lobbying of Congress by corporations winning Bank contracts'.[41]

Similar incentives propelled lending by commercial banks, with the added spark of the profit motive. Much private credit took the form of syndicated loans, a financial innovation dating from petrodollar recycling in the wake of the OPEC oil price increases of the 1970s. Syndicated loans drew funds from groups ('syndicates') of banks that were organized on a loan-by-loan basis by lead banks, typically headquartered in New York, London or Paris. Many of these loans had floating interest rates indexed to the London Interbank Offered Rate (Libor), the rate at which banks lend to each other. Some examples of syndicated loans are given in Table 1.1.

The spread – the difference between the interest rate charged to the borrowing country and Libor – brought profits to the syndicate participants over the term of the loan. But more immediate gratification came upfront in the form of loan origination fees. These could be booked as profits in the same financial quarter that the loan was issued. A 1.5 per cent fee on a $100 million loan would amount to $1.5 million, a tidy sum. This was taken off the top from the money disbursed to the borrower. The lead banks passed a slice of this upfront money – formally known as a 'participation fee' – to other syndicate members, the percentage slice varying with the size of their commitment.[42] Bankers informally called these participation fees 'juicers'.

In *Selling Money*, an illuminating account of his experiences as an international loan officer for regional American banks in the 1970s and early 1980s, S. C. Gwynne recalls receiving a stream of telexes from lead banks seeking to 'sell down' participation in syndicated loans. 'The volume of such telexes at Cleveland Trust was astonishing in those years,' he recalls. 'It was common to arrive at the office and find a pile of "bedsheet" telexes covering my desk, offering millions of dollars in loan participations, all wanting quick replies.'[43]

'Many of the participating banks', according to syndication expert Robert P. McDonald of Chase Manhattan, 'had no firm understanding of whom they were lending to; very few performed any type of credit analysis and practically none had a tactical and/ or strategic marketing plan delineated by geography.'[44]

'Volume', Gwynne remarks, 'was all that mattered.'[45]

Export promotion entered into lending decisions by commercial banks, too, when the exporters who stood to benefit from

TABLE 1.1 Examples of syndicated loans

Country	Year	Amount	Lead and manager banks
Zaire	1974	$22,264,043	American Express International Banking Corporation Crédit Commercial de France
Sudan	1974	$200,000,000	Crédit Commercial de France Banque Nationale de Paris Banque Arabe et Internationale d'Investissement
Gabon	1976	$20,000,000	American Express International Banking Corporation Citicorp International Bank Ltd Wells Fargo Bank International
Côte d'Ivoire	1976	$50,000,000	Citicorp International Bank Ltd Brandts Ltd Chase Manhattan Ltd Amex Bank Ltd Bank of Montreal First Chicago Ltd Merrill Lynch International Bank Ltd
Kenya	1979	$200,000,000	National Westminster Bank Group Bank of Montreal Bank of Tokyo Ltd Barclays International Group Chase Manhattan Banking Group Citicorp International Group Deutsche Bank Compagnie Financière Luxembourg First Chicago Ltd Fuji Bank Ltd Manufacturers Hanover Ltd Midland Bank Ltd Royal Bank of Canada Standard Chartered Bank
Nigeria	1981	$308,000,000	Midland Bank Ltd BankAmerica International Group Barclays Bank Group Crocker National Bank Fuji Bank Ltd Mitsui Trust and Banking Company Ltd Orion Royal Bank Ltd

Source: Tombstones appearing in *Euromoney*, June 1974, pp. 45, 74; May 1976, p. 71; August 1976, p. 3; August 1979, p. 54; December 1981, p. 125

the loan were important bank customers. For example, Gwynne recounts how the Cleveland Trust Company was drawn into the international lending business: 'As a big-league corporate bank, Cleveland Trust had big-league corporate clients, and most of these clients had significant overseas operations.' These clients 'not only needed but expected the bank to finance their international trade'.[46]

As long as juicy fees were flowing freely, few bankers worried much about future repayment difficulties. Citibank chairman Walter Wriston assured his fellow bankers that 'sovereign nations don't go bankrupt'.[47] Meanwhile, successful young loan officers moved from bank to bank, leapfrogging up the salary scale. If the quality of loans eventually turned out to be a problem, they could rest easy in the knowledge that by that time it would be someone else's problem.

The perverse incentives for pushing loans to Africa and other developing countries in Latin America and Asia sound eerily familiar in the wake of the 2008 subprime mortgage meltdown in the United States, which triggered the world's worst economic crisis since the depression of the 1930s. The incentives in the US financial system that spawned this crisis bear a close resemblance to those that drove profligate lending to developing countries in the 1970s and 1980s. For subprime mortgage lenders in the USA, the overriding aim again was to move the money. 'They didn't care about the quality of the mortgage,' explains Professor Nouriel Roubini of New York University. 'They were caring about maximizing their volume, and getting a fee out of it.'[48]

Once again, the intoxicating appeal of upfront fees pushed any concerns about loan repayment difficulties out of sight and out of mind. 'As long as the music is playing, you've got to get up and dance,' the chief executive officer of Citigroup merrily explained to the *Financial Times* in 2007. 'We're still dancing.'[49]

Once again, short-run greed trumped long-run prudence. 'The profits from reckless activities were simply too tantalizing and titanic to pass up for many of the executives running these institutions,' explains Gretchen Morgenson, financial correspondent

27

of the *New York Times*. 'The take-the-money-and-run mentality ran amok.'[50]

Perverse incentives are not confined to the lender side of international credit markets, as we have seen. On the borrower side, too, foreign loans were subject to what economists call a 'principal-agent' problem: an agent who is supposed to act on behalf of others (the principals) instead may put his own self-interest first. In loans to Africa and other developing nations, the people were the principals and top government officials were the agents. Officials borrowed in the name of the government, lined their own pockets and those of their cronies, and left the people with the debts.

Diverse methods were used to channel funds from foreign loans to African governments into private pockets. We have already seen several examples: kickbacks and padded procurement contracts in Nigeria, oil-backed loans in the Republic of Congo, direct transfers from public accounts in Gabon. Another popular technique was public expenditure for 'ghosts' – fictitious roads, schools, soldiers, and so on. In Uganda, for example, officials reported in 2010 that medical supplies were being ostensibly delivered to some hundred non-existent facilities, including seven 'ghost hospitals' in the capital, Kampala.[51]

Having diverted borrowed funds into their own pockets by such ruses, well-connected Africans could readily find foreign bankers who were willing and able to assist in moving the loot into hidden accounts abroad. In doing so, they took advantage of bank secrecy jurisdictions, also known as 'tax havens' – the same network of financial institutions that is used not only by narcotics traffickers and other criminals seeking to hide their profits but also by large corporations seeking to evade taxation. The players in the international tax haven network include major banks. Citigroup, for example, has 427 subsidiaries in 'tax havens or financial privacy jurisdictions' around the world, according to a 2008 report by the US Government Accountability Office, including ninety in the Cayman Islands alone.[52]

The term 'capital flight' focuses attention on the exodus of

To Walter Wriston
with best wishes,

Ronald Reagan

4 Citibank chairman Walter Wriston offered the assurance that 'sovereign nations don't go bankrupt' (Tufts University, Digital Collections and Archives)

funds from African countries, but as financial journalist Nicholas Shaxson remarks in his book *Treasure Islands*, 'each flight of capital out of Africa must have a corresponding inflow somewhere else'.[53] The bankers who provide safe havens for flight capital again reap lucrative spreads and fees for their services. At a conference on capital flight and Third World debt held in Washington, DC, in 1986, Austrian banker Erhard Fürst observed that foreign depositors in Swiss banks often received negative interest returns, 'implying that they were willing to pay a substantial premium for security'.[54]

In these respects, too, the pathologies of international finance have not been confined to Africa and other low-income nations. 'The lines between thievery and patriotism, between private advantage and the national interest, became impossibly blurred,' wrote Fintan O'Toole in his 2010 book *Ship of Fools*.[55] O'Toole was writing not about Nigeria, or Congo, or Gabon, but about the debt crisis engulfing his own country, Ireland.

Africa's debt trap

The 1998 World Bank study's conclusion that much aid to developing countries went into poorly managed economies 'with little result' is only half true. Multimillion-dollar loans always have results, even if not the ones that were ostensibly intended.

One notable result of the lax lending by official and private creditors to Africa has been the phenomenon of debt-fuelled capital flight. Some of this flight capital wound up in private accounts at the same banks that arranged the loans. 'The borrowers stole the money and the lenders helped them steal it,' in the blunt words of Brookings Institution scholar Raymond Baker. 'In my judgment this is the ugliest chapter in international commerce since slavery.'[56]

This dual bank–client relationship is illustrated in the case of Gabon by President Omar Bongo's personal accounts at BNP, Crédit Lyonnais and Citibank. All three banks played important roles in syndicated loans to the government (see the 'tombstones' reproduced in Figure 1.1). In the next two chapters we document

$15,000,000

Ten Year Loan

to

L'Office du Chemin de Fer Transgabonais

Guaranteed by

The Republic of Gabon

Arranged by

Loeb, Rhoades & Co.

Citicorp International Bank Limited

Banque Internationale Pour L'Afrique Occidentale S. A.

Provided by

Bank of Montreal	Banque Canadienne Nationale
Banque Commerciale Pour L'Europe du Nord (Eurobank)	
Banque Internationale Pour L'Afrique Occidentale S.A.	
Banque de L'Union Européenne S.A.	Chemical Bank
Citicorp International Bank Limited	The Fidelity Bank
First National City Bank	First National Bank of Chicago
First Pennsylvania Overseas Development Company (Cayman) Ltd.	
National and Grindlays Bank Limited	

June 18, 1974

GABONESE REPUBLIC

15,000,000 U.S. $ 10 ¼ % BONDS DUE 1980

SOCIÉTÉ GÉNÉRALE   BANQUE DE SUEZ ET DE L'UNION DES MINES

BERLINER HANDELS- UND FRANKFURTER BANK

SOCIÉTÉ FINANCIÈRE POUR LE MOYEN-ORIENT - SOFIMO S.A.L.

SOCIÉTÉ GÉNÉRALE DE BANQUE S.A.

BANQUE BRUXELLES LAMBERT S.A.   BANQUE NATIONALE DE PARIS

CRÉDIT LYONNAIS

ALAHLI BANK OF KUWAIT S.A.K.
ARAB FINANCE CORP. S.A.L.
ASSOCIATED JAPANESE BANK (INTERNATIONAL) LIMITED
BANCA NAZIONALE DEL LAVORO
BANK GUTZWILLER, KURZ, BUNGENER (OVERSEAS) LIMITED
BANQUE FRANÇAISE DU COMMERCE EXTÉRIEUR
BANQUE WORMS
BROWN HARRIMAN & INTERNATIONAL BANKS LTD
CAISSE DES DÉPÔTS ET CONSIGNATIONS
CREDIT SUISSE WHITE WELD LIMITED
CREDITO ITALIANO
ANTONY GIBBS HOLDINGS LTD.
HALSEY STUART & CO. INC.
ISTITUTO BANCARIO SAN PAOLO DI TORINO
Affiliate of Bache & Co. Inc.
JAPAN INTERNATIONAL BANK LIMITED
KUWAIT INTERNATIONAL INVESTMENT CO. S.A.K.
MANUFACTURERS HANOVER LIMITED
B. METZLER SEEL. SOHN UND CO
NORDDEUTSCHE LANDESBANK GIROZENTRALE
PIERSON, HELDRING & PIERSON
SALOMON BROTHERS
SCANDINAVIAN BANK LIMITED
SKANDINAVISKA ENSKILDA BANKEN
SMITH, BARNEY & CO. INCORPORATED
SOCIÉTÉ GÉNÉRALE ALSACIENNE DE BANQUE
SOCIÉTÉ SEQUANAISE DE BANQUE
VEREINS- UND WESTBANK AKTIENGESELLSCHAFT

SOCIÉTÉ INTERCONTINENTALE DE BANQUE, Luxembourg, acted as advisor of the managers.

1.1 Examples of tombstones announcing syndicated loans to Gabon. *Source: Euromoney,* October 1975, p. 34; July 1974, p. 86.

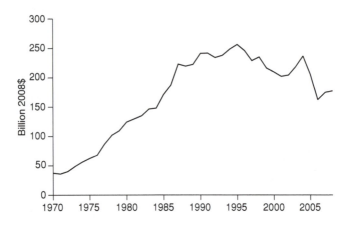

1.2 Total debt stock, thirty-three sub-Saharan African countries ($ billion, in constant 2008 dollars) *Source*: World Bank, World Development Indicators and Global Development Finance database. Converted to 2008 dollars using the GDP deflator as reported in the World Bank's World Development Indicators.

the magnitude of African capital flight and its relationship to foreign loans.

A second, and more evident, result of subprime lending to Africa was the accumulation of large foreign debts. This has resulted in the ongoing drain of the continent's scarce resources into external debt service payments.

The total foreign debt of the thirty-three sub-Saharan African countries analysed in this book – those for which adequate data are available – is shown in Figure 1.2. Here and throughout the book we use 2008 dollars so as to depict real trends without the distorting effects of inflation. From less than $50 billion (in 2008 dollars) in 1970, the debt rose sharply through the late 1980s, and then more gradually until it peaked at over $250 billion in 1995. Since then the debt stock has declined to about $180 billion, owing to debt repayments and write-offs coupled with relatively modest new lending.

The composition of sub-Saharan Africa's external debt by type is shown in Figure 1.3. In 2008, roughly half the total was long-term debt to official creditors: 22 per cent was held by bilateral

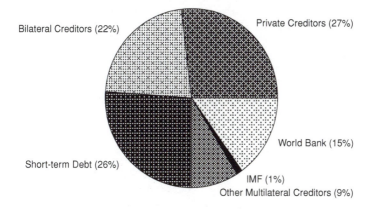

Bilateral Creditors (22%)

Private Creditors (27%)

World Bank (15%)

Short-term Debt (26%)

IMF (1%)

Other Multilateral Creditors (9%)

1.3 Debt by creditor in sub-Saharan Africa, 2008 *Source*: World Bank, World Development Indicators and Global Development Finance database

creditors; 15 per cent by the World Bank; 1 per cent by the IMF; and 9 per cent by other official multilateral creditors. Another 27 per cent was held by private creditors as long-term debt; and an additional 26 per cent was short-term debt, most of it also owed to private creditors.[57]

The composition of Africa's debt has varied over time. The share of private creditors peaked on the eve of the debt crisis that struck developing countries in 1983, which led to a sharp contraction of new lending by commercial banks. Private long-term debt shrank from 36 per cent of the total in 1982 to only 18 per cent in 2004, after which its share rose, mainly by virtue of write-offs of bilateral debts by official creditors. Since 1983, new loans have come mostly from the official creditors, allowing African countries to service their debts to private creditors, paying them off or at least slowing the rate at which they fell into arrears. In effect, public money from the governments of industrialized countries thus helped to bail out the private creditors – again presaging a pattern that would recur in the wake of the subprime crisis in the United States.[58] Meanwhile capital flight from Africa continued, as we document in the next chapter. 'It is the Western taxpayers who are paying it out over the table,' Raymond Baker explained to a *New York Times* reporter in 1999, 'and the private banks who take it back under the table.'[59]

The ten sub-Saharan African countries with the largest external debts in 2008 are listed in Table 1.2. South Africa tops the list with an external debt of almost $42 billion, followed by Sudan, Angola, Côte d'Ivoire, the Democratic Republic of Congo and Nigeria, all of which owed more than $10 billion. Debts for each of the thirty-three countries covered in this book are reported in Appendix Table A.1, together with the ratio of external debts to gross domestic product (GDP). In several countries debt exceeds GDP, with Zimbabwe having the dubious distinction of the highest ratio at 186 per cent.

TABLE 1.2 External debt: the top ten (sub-Saharan African countries, 2008)

Country	US$ billion
South Africa	41.9
Sudan	19.6
Angola	15.1
Côte d'Ivoire	12.6
Congo, Dem. Rep.	12.2
Nigeria	11.2
Kenya	7.4
Tanzania	5.9
Congo, Rep.	5.5
Zimbabwe	5.2

Source: World Bank, World Development Indicators and Global Development Finance database

As Africa's external debt grew, so did its outflow of debt service: interest payments and principal repayment. Figure 1.4 shows the trend in debt service payments since the early 1970s, again in constant 2008 dollars. From less than $1 billion per year in the early 1970s, debt service payments from the thirty-three sub-Saharan African countries have risen to more than $10 billion per year since 1994, with a peak outflow of $20 billion in 2006.

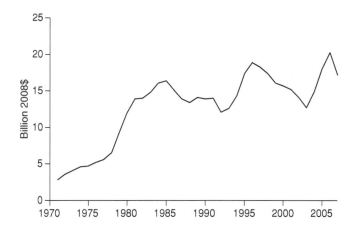

1.4 External debt service payments ($ billion, in constant 2008 dollars; three-year moving average) *Source*: World Bank, World Development Indicators and Global Development Finance database

Figure 1.5 shows the trend in net transfers for all thirty-three countries in the same period. The net transfer is the difference between inflows from new borrowing and outflows from debt service payments on past loans. Positive net transfers to Africa –

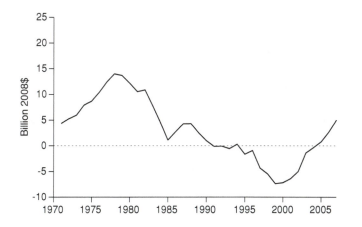

1.5 Net transfer ($ billion, in constant 2008 dollars; three-year moving average) *Source*: World Bank, World Development Indicators and Global Development Finance database

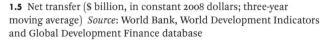

Tales from the shadows

when new money exceeds debt service payments – peaked in the late 1970s. For the past quarter-century, however, the average value of the net transfer to sub-Saharan Africa has been approximately zero. In other words, the inflows from new international lending have roughly offset the outflows to service debts incurred in earlier years.

When a country experiences a *negative* net transfer – as has happened to many African nations since the mid-1990s – it actually pays more in debt service than it receives in new money. In such periods, foreign loans are a net drain on the economy, siphoning resources away from investment and consumption. For example, in the period 2000–08, the Democratic Republic of Congo (former Zaire) experienced a negative net transfer of $1.4 billion. Over this same period, the negative net transfer from the Republic of Congo amounted to $1.2 billion; from Gabon it was $4.2 billion. Nigeria saw a negative net transfer of more than $20 billion from 2000 until its 2006 Paris Club debt deal, on top of a $16 billion negative net transfer in the previous decade.[60]

The negative net transfer is not merely a possibility: it is a mathematical certainty, in the absence of debt write-offs. Loans must be repaid with interest. For a time, a rising tide of new lending can enable borrowers to meet their debt service obligations with money to spare, resulting in a positive net transfer. But African countries, like individuals, cannot borrow ever-larger sums for ever. When the new money fails to cover debt service payments on old money, the era of negative net transfers begins.

If foreign loans were invested productively, yielding a rate of return sufficient to repay them with interest, a country's economy would still be better off during the era of negative net transfers than if it had never borrowed. But if, instead, the loans were squandered on ill-conceived projects or diverted into capital flight, the country is worse off once the net transfer turns negative than if it had never borrowed in the first place. In Africa, the latter has not been the exception but the rule.

For some African countries, the burden of negative net transfers has been eased if not eliminated by 'debt relief' offered by creditors. For example, French president François Mitterrand announced in 1989 that France would write off $2.6 billion in bilateral debts owed by low-income African countries.[61] Some countries, such as Nigeria, have negotiated debt write-downs from the Paris Club of official creditors as a whole. Such concessions contributed to the modest decline in sub-Saharan Africa's total debt since the mid-1990s, shown in Figure 1.2, although the conditions attached by creditors to debt relief have often been controversial.[62] More importantly, for the purposes of the present book, debt write-offs do not address the fundamental weaknesses in international finance that generated repayment problems in the first place. Debt relief can treat the symptoms, but not the disease.

2 | Measuring African capital flight

In March 2010, the African Union and the UN Economic Commission for Africa jointly convened the annual Conference of African Ministers of Finance in Lilongwe, Malawi, around the theme of 'Promoting high level sustainable growth to reduce unemployment in Africa'. The agenda included a high-level session on 'the phenomenon of illicit financial flows from Africa and its devastating impact on development prospects'.[1] This reflected increasing recognition that capital flight poses a major development challenge for African countries. The issue is at the heart of discussions of development finance, transparency in public resource management, and the sustainability of external borrowing.

The magnitude of African capital flight is staggering both in absolute monetary values and relative to GDP. For the thirty-three sub-Saharan African countries for which we have data, we find that more than $700 billion fled the continent between 1970 and 2008. If this capital was invested abroad and earned interest at the going market rates, the accumulated capital loss for these countries over the thirty-nine-year period was $944 billion. By comparison, total GDP for all of sub-Saharan Africa in 2008 stood at $997 billion.[2]

Comparisons to Asia and Latin America have found that capital flight from Africa is smaller in sheer dollar terms, but larger relative to the size of the African economy.[3]

Reading the hidden balance of payments

Measurement of capital flight poses daunting challenges, and requires some rather sophisticated statistical detective work. Funds that are acquired illegally, or funnelled abroad illegally, or both, are not entered into the official accounts of African countries. At the same time, the perpetrators of capital flight benefit from the complicity of bankers and other operators who assist in the placement of the funds in foreign havens. The identities of asset holders are often concealed through proxies and by taking advantage of legal screens available in bank secrecy jurisdictions. Nevertheless, researchers have made substantial progress in developing ways to estimate the magnitude of capital flight. This section reviews the methods used in this book.[4]

Residual measures of capital flight Our starting point is the balance of payments (BoP), each country's official record of inflows and outflows of foreign exchange. These data are compiled annually by the IMF on the basis of reports from the central banks of its member governments. The 'current account' of the BoP records international flows arising from trade in goods and services, interest payments and transfers – transactions that do not lead to future claims on resources. The 'capital account' records flows of loans, investments and other financial transactions that entail future claims. Outflows of foreign exchange to the rest of the world, such as debt service or payments for imports, are recorded as debits (denoted by a negative sign). Inflows, such as loan disbursements or payments for exports, are recorded as credits (with a positive sign).[5] The net sum of the current account and the capital account gives the country's overall BoP position, which in principle corresponds to the net change in the country's official reserves of foreign exchange. A BoP surplus, when foreign exchange inflows exceed outflows, translates into a gain in international reserves. A BoP deficit, when outflows exceed inflows, translates into a loss of reserves. In practice, recorded inflows and outflows of foreign exchange seldom match exactly the changes in the country's official foreign exchange reserves. The missing money, or residual, is labelled 'net errors and omissions' in the BoP.

In the wake of the 1983 Third World debt crisis, it was discovered that the inflows of foreign borrowing recorded in the official BoP were often understated by substantial amounts. As a result, the total stock of external debt, built up over years of borrowing, often exceeded the cumulative borrowing as reported

39

in the BoP. The World Bank independently assembles annual data on the stock of debt. This information, contained in a World Bank database called *Global Development Finance* (GDF), provides the basis for corrections to the BoP figures. By taking GDF data on changes in debt stocks, substituting this for the BoP data on foreign borrowing, and recalculating net errors and omissions, we can obtain a new residual estimate of missing money. The World Bank (1985) and others pioneered this technique to derive a measure of capital flight.[6]

In recalculating debt inflows from the change in debt stock as reported in GDF, it can be important to take into account the fact that although the end-of-year debt stock is reported in US dollars, debts are denominated in various other hard currencies, too, such as the euro, the British pound and the Japanese yen. Hence the change-in-debt measure of inflows must be adjusted for the impact of exchange rate fluctuations during the year on the total debt outstanding.[7]

Trade misinvoicing as a source of capital flight In addition to incomplete recording of debt inflows, another well-known source of errors in the official BoP accounts is trade misinvoicing. This can take several forms. Both importers and exporters may manipulate the reported values of their transactions in order to conceal foreign exchange transactions from the country's monetary authorities. In the case of exporters, under-invoicing (by falsely under-reporting the quantity of goods exported and/or the price received) evades tax liabilities and reduces the amount of foreign exchange that must be surrendered to the authorities from export receipts. In the case of importers, over-invoicing (by inflating the quantity and/or price of imports) increases the amount of foreign exchange they can obtain on favourable terms from the central bank to pay for imports. Both export under-invoicing and import over-invoicing are important mechanisms for capital flight. When exporters understate the value of their export revenues, they often retain abroad the difference between the true value and the declared value. Similarly, when importers send extra foreign exchange abroad, ostensibly to pay for imports, the excess (minus a commission for their partners) is often deposited in a designated foreign bank account.

On the import side, a further source of error in the official BoP statistics arises from efforts to evade customs duties and restrictions. In the case of outright ('pure') smuggling, the value of the imports goes completely unrecorded. In the case of 'technical' smuggling, import quantities and/or prices are understated in order to reduce import duties. Of course, the imports must be paid for, regardless of whether or to what extent they are reported to customs officials. Both types of smuggling therefore result in the understatement of foreign exchange outflows in the BoP.[8]

The net impact of trade misinvoicing on the BoP depends on the relative importance of these different forms. The current account deficit reported in the BoP is inflated by export under-invoicing and import over-invoicing; it is deflated by import under-invoicing. The simple residual measure of capital flight will be too low if the true current account deficit is overstated, as some capital flight is hidden in the trade accounts. Conversely, the simple residual measure of capital flight will be too high if the true current account deficit is understated: some of the missing foreign exchange was, in fact, used to finance unrecorded imports. The net effect of trade misinvoicing cannot be determined on the basis of a priori reasoning; it can only be ascertained empirically.[9]

The extent of trade misinvoicing can be estimated by comparing the export and import data provided by an African country to the corresponding import and export data of its trading partners. Both sets of figures are reported in another annual IMF publication, *Direction of Trade Statistics*. If we assume that the trade data provided to the IMF by the industrialized countries are relatively accurate, the discrepancy between these figures and the data from their African trading partners yields a measure of trade misinvoicing. For each African country, we compute export discrepancies with the industrialized countries as the difference between the value of industrialized countries' imports from the African country as reported by industrialized countries, and

41

the African country's exports to industrialized countries as reported by the African country (with an adjustment to account for the costs of freight and insurance). A positive difference indicates export under-invoicing. Similarly, import discrepancies with the industrialized countries are calculated as the difference between the African country's imports from industrialized countries as reported by the African country, and the industrialized countries' exports to the African country as reported by the industrialized countries. A positive difference indicates net over-invoicing of imports; a negative sign indicates net under-invoicing. Because the industrialized countries do not account for all of the African country's trade, we obtain a global total misinvoicing estimate by scaling up these discrepancies (multiplying them by the inverse of the average shares of industrialized countries in the African country's exports and imports).

As we show in the next section, adjustment for the effects of trade misinvoicing leads to substantial net additions to total capital flight in some countries in some years. This result is consistent with the findings of other studies.[10]

Discrepancies in workers' remittances One more item in the BoP statistics that can be an important source of error is workers' remittances. Over the past few decades, many African countries have recorded large and increasing inflows of remittances from their citizens who are working in other African countries, Europe and, to a lesser extent, the United States and other industrialized countries. In some African countries, remittances are now larger than conventional external financing from aid or foreign direct investment. However, a substantial fraction of remittance inflows is transferred through informal channels that escape recording in official BoP statistics. The World Bank estimates that unrecorded remittances in African countries account for more than half of total remittance inflows.[11]

Adjusting for remittance discrepancies is important for accurate measurement of capital flight, as the unrecorded inflows increase the amount of foreign exchange that is available to the country. The effect of unrecorded remittances thus is similar to that of unreported export earnings: the amount of foreign exchange actually entering the African country is greater than what is captured in the official BoP.

Unrecorded remittances are typically exchanged for local currency in the informal banking system, and the hard currency is then sold to others who use it for a variety of purposes, only one of which may be capital flight. The foreign exchange could also be used, for example, to pay for unrecorded imports. The actual use of the remittances does not matter for capital flight measurement, since capital flight is computed as a residual: the difference between total foreign exchange inflows and all other uses of foreign exchange (including changes in official reserves), after the balance-of-payments accounts have been adjusted on the basis of more accurate data on foreign borrowing and trade in goods and services as well as remittances.

The International Fund for Agricultural Development (IFAD) has computed alternative measures of workers' remittance inflows by using survey data.[12] The IFAD estimates were derived by combining data on total numbers and locations of migrant workers in 2006 with survey data for various host-origin country pairs on the percentage of migrants who send remittances and the average amount sent. The results indicate that the true magnitude of remittance inflows to Africa is substantially underestimated in the BoP data. For example, IFAD estimates that remittance inflows from industrialized countries to Nigeria in 2006 amounted to $5.4 billion, compared to $3.3 billion reported in the official BoP statistics. For Angola, the BoP reports no remittances whatsoever in that year, whereas the IFAD estimate shows an inflow of $969 million.

We estimate the volume of unreported remittances by comparing the IFAD estimates of inflows from industrialized countries to the total inflows from all countries recorded in the official BoP statistics.[13] In principle, the latter should be larger since they should include remittances from the entire world, not only from the industrialized countries.[14] Where, instead, the former exceeds the latter, we take this to be strong evidence of under-reporting.

TABLE 2.1 Measuring capital flight (example: Angola in the year 2008)

	$ million
New borrowing: change in external debt outstanding, adjusted for changes in the debt stock due to write-offs and exchange-rate effects on its dollar value (*source*: World Bank, Global Development Finance)	3,655
Plus	+
Net foreign direct investment (*source*: World Bank, World Development Indicators)	1,679
Minus	−
Current account deficit (negative sign indicates a surplus) (*source*: IMF, Balance of Payments Statistics)	− 6,408
Minus	−
Changes in reserves and related items (positive sign indicates addition to reserves) (*source*: IMF, Balance of Payments Statistics)	5,610
Equals	=
Residual measure of Angolan capital flight (subtotal before adjustments	6,132
Plus	+
Adjustment for export misinvoicing (positive sign reflects under-invoicing) (*source*: IMF, Direction of Trade Statistics)	537
Plus	+
Adjustment for import misinvoicing (positive sign indicates net over-invoicing; negative sign would indicate net under-invoicing [smuggling]) (*source*: IMF, Direction of Trade Statistics)	172
Plus	+
Adjustment for unrecorded remittances (see text for method of calculation)	804
Equals	=
ANGOLAN CAPITAL FLIGHT IN 2008	7,645

We calculate the discrepancy for the year 2006 (the only year for which IFAD's alternative estimates are available), and extrapolate from this to estimate discrepancies for other years based on the trend in overall African remittance inflows reported in the BoP statistics. We adjust our measure of capital flight by adding into it the value of the remittance discrepancy.

In Table 2.1 we illustrate these calculations using data from Angola for the year 2008. In that year, Angola received $3,655 million in new borrowing, plus a net inflow of $1,679 million in foreign direct investment. From these capital inflows we subtract the uses of foreign exchange recorded in the official balance-of-payments statistics: the current account deficit (in this instance, it was a surplus of $6,408 million), and additions to official foreign exchange reserves ($5,610 million). This gives the unadjusted residual measure of capital flight: $6,132 million. Adding the adjustments for trade misinvoicing and unrecorded remittances brings total capital flight from Angola in that year to $7,645 million.

Adjustments for inflation and interest earnings To obtain measures for the period from 1970 to 2008, the final step is to convert the annual flows into figures that are comparable across different years, since a dollar outflow in 1970 is not the same as a dollar outflow in 2008. In principle, this can be done either by adjusting for inflation (that is, converting nominal dollars into real terms expressed in a constant base-year value) or by imputing interest earnings on capital that fled in earlier years.[15] As long as the real interest rate is positive, the cumulative stock of flight capital will be higher when calculated by the second adjustment.

The choice of the method used to adjust the nominal capital flight series depends on the intended use of the data. The real (inflation-adjusted) annual values are appropriate for the analysis of trends, causes and consequences of capital flight. The interest-adjusted stock of capital flight is more appropriate for assessing the opportunity cost of capital flight, which includes forgone earnings on the lost resources, and for comparing cumulative capital flight to the stock of external debt (which includes capitalized interest arrears and borrowing to cover interest payments). In the following section, we present both real values of annual capital flight adjusted for inflation, and stocks of capital flight adjusted for imputed interest earnings.

45

Counting the missing money

Using the method described above, we estimated the amount of capital flight from thirty-three sub-Saharan African countries for which adequate data are available for most years.[16] The numbers are eye-opening. Total capital flight from these countries over the 1970–2008 period (in 2008 US dollars) amounted to $735 billion. This is equivalent to roughly 80 per cent of the combined GDP of these countries in 2008. As can be seen in Figure 2.1, while annual capital flight was highest in the last seven years of this period, the phenomenon is not new. This indicates that capital flight from African countries is not a transitory product of unusual circumstances, but rather an outcome of persistent underlying causes.

If the funds that left African countries during this period were invested in assets that earned the interest rate on short-term US Treasury bills, the cumulative stock of flight capital with imputed interest earnings in 2008 would amount to $944 billion.

In practice, of course, the fate of the missing money in most cases is unknown. Undoubtedly some of it was not invested, but

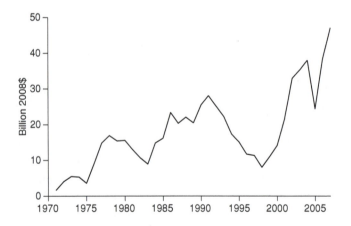

2.1 Annual capital flight for thirty-three sub-Saharan African countries, 1970–2008 ($ billion, in constant 2008 dollars; three-year moving average) *Source*: Authors' computations

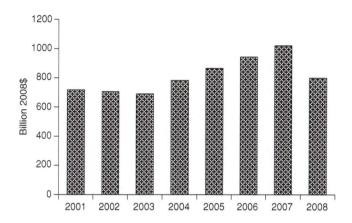

2.2 Wealth of Africa's high net worth individuals *Source*: Capgemini and Merrill Lynch Wealth Management, World Wealth Report (2004: 8; 2007: 3; 2009: 3). Converted to 2008 dollars using the GDP deflator as reported in the World Bank's World Development Indicators.

instead was dissipated in Parisian shopping sprees and other consumption. On the other hand, some may have yielded returns above the fairly conservative US Treasury bill rate. Whatever the rate of return that accrued on average to African flight capital, its cumulative stock with imputed interest earnings is a reasonable indicator of the opportunity cost of the failure to invest these funds productively in Africa. It also provides the most appropriate measure for comparison to Africa's external debts, since these accrue interest regardless of how the borrowed money was used.

Our $944 billion estimate of the cumulative stock of African flight capital closely matches the total wealth of Africa's high net worth individuals (HNWIs) as reported in *World Wealth Report*, an annual publication of the financial services firms Capgemini and Merrill Lynch Global Wealth Management which tracks the holdings of HNWIs around the globe. The report defines HNWIs as people with investable personal assets of $1 million or more. The total wealth of Africa's HNWIs peaked, according to this source, at $1 trillion in 2007 before slipping to $800 billion in 2008 as a result of the global financial crisis (see Figure 2.2).[17]

TABLE 2.2 African capital flight: the top ten

Country	Total real capital flight ($ billion, in constant 2008 dollars)	Ratio of real capital flight to 2008 GDP (%)	Total capital flight stock with interest, 2008 ($ billion)	External debt, 2008 ($ billion)	Net external assets, 2008 ($ billion)
Nigeria	296.2	139.7	376.9	11.2	365.6
Angola	71.5	85.8	80.0	15.1	64.8
Côte d'Ivoire	45.4	194.1	66.2	12.6	53.7
South Africa	36.2	13.1	36.4	41.9	-5.5
Democratic Republic of Congo	30.7	265.1	48.4	12.2	36.2
Zambia	24.4	170.5	35.1	3.0	32.1
Cameroon	24.0	102.8	33.3	2.8	30.5
Republic of Congo	23.9	223.4	26.9	5.5	21.4
Zimbabwe	22.6	807.6	31.3	5.2	26.1
Ethiopia	20.1	76.0	26.0	2.9	23.1
Total for 33 countries	734.9	80.8	944.2	176.9	767.3

Source: Authors' computations

Inter-country comparisons Some African countries have suffered more than others from the financial haemorrhage of capital flight. Table 2.2 presents our estimates for the ten countries with the greatest capital flight in sheer dollar terms; data for all thirty-three countries are presented in Appendix Table A.2. Topping the list are Nigeria (with $296 billion of capital flight over the period, in 2008 dollars), Angola ($72 billion) and Côte d'Ivoire ($46 billion). Six of the top ten are oil-rich countries (Angola, Nigeria, Côte d'Ivoire, Republic of Congo, Democratic Republic of Congo and Cameroon). This raises the question of linkages between capital flight and the exploitation of natural resources in African countries, an issue to which we return in Chapter 3.

Focusing on the dollar amount of capital flight may give a misleading sense of relative burdens, since in smaller economies even a modest outflow could represent a substantial drain. For example, total capital flight over the period was equivalent to 614 per cent of the 2008 GDP for São Tomé and Príncipe, 493 per cent for Seychelles, 384 per cent for Burundi, and 312 per cent for Sierra Leone. By this measure the burden of capital flight was substantial for a number of large economies, too: 807 per cent of 2008 GDP for Zimbabwe, 265 per cent for the Democratic Republic of Congo, 223 per cent for the Republic of Congo, and 194 per cent for Côte d'Ivoire.

Trade misinvoicing as a conduit for capital flight One conduit for capital flight, as discussed above, is trade misinvoicing. When exporters understate their true exports earnings, and importers overstate the true costs of their imports, they obtain foreign exchange that can be held abroad. On the other hand, payments for unrecorded imports require foreign exchange expenditures that likewise go unrecorded in the official balance-of-payments accounts. Hence the net effect of adjustments to capital flight estimates for trade misinvoicing can go in either direction.

On the export side, under-invoicing over the 1970–2008 period totalled $312 billion (in 2008 dollars) in the thirty-three sub-Saharan African countries studied here. It is clear, therefore, that export under-invoicing has been a major conduit for African capital flight.

Country-level studies have indicated that natural resource sectors can be especially prone to this phenomenon. A recent study on South Africa, for example, finds that most of the country's trade misinvoicing happens in exports of ores and metals.[18] To some extent the importance of export under-invoicing in natural resource sectors simply reflects their large share in African exports, but it also may be due to specific characteristics of these sectors, such as the opacity of transactions and the involvement of politically powerful individuals and firms.

On the import side, the net effect of misinvoicing on our capital flight estimates varied among countries. In some cases, over-invoicing (for capital flight) outweighed smuggling (for evasion of customs duties); in other cases, the reverse was true. In aggregate the smuggling effect predominated, resulting in net under-invoicing of $135 billion over the period.

It should be noted, however, that this result does *not* imply that import over-invoicing for capital flight was an unimportant conduit for capital flight. The following hypothetical example will make this clear. Suppose that capital flight via import over-invoicing amounted to $300 billion – a sum comparable to capital flight via export under-invoicing – and that smuggling concealed $435 billion in payments for imports. The combination would yield net import under-invoicing of $135 million, resulting in a corresponding downward adjustment of our capital flight estimates. We cannot ascertain the separate effects of both types of import misinvoicing, as our data reveal only their net effect.

Taken together, the two trade misinvoicing adjustments – on the export side and the import side – add $177 billion to our unadjusted residual measure of capital flight: export under-invoicing adds $312 billion, while net import under-invoicing subtracts $135 billion (see Table 2.3).

Again, there are substantial variations across countries in the magnitude and pattern of trade misinvoicing. To illustrate, we report details for four countries in Table 2.3. The Nigerian

TABLE 2.3 Adjustments for trade misinvoicing and remittance discrepancies (1970–2008; $ million, in constant 2008 dollars)

Country	Unadjusted residual measure of capital flight	Trade misinvoicing			Remittance discrepancies	Total capital flight
		Exports	Imports	Net		
All 33 countries	432,159.2	311,838.0	−134,765.3	177,055.7	125,699.3	734,914.2
Nigeria	208,236.2	76,288.1	−6,973.8	69,314.3	18,670.3	296,220.8
Côte d'Ivoire	31,396.1	11,391.0	877.1	12,268.1	1,790.1	45,454.3
Ethiopia	23,636.3	1,199.2	−10,280.3	−9,081.1	5,567.5	20,122.7
Angola	59,129.4	584.8	−49.9	534.9	11,848.7	71,513.0

Source: Authors' computations

case is representative of the overall pattern: substantial export under-invoicing, coupled with substantial but less dramatic net under-invoicing on the import side. Côte d'Ivoire illustrates a second pattern, in which import under-invoicing outweighs smuggling, thereby increasing the trade misinvoicing adjustment to our capital flight estimates. Ethiopia illustrates a third variant: here the use of foreign exchange to pay for smuggled imports dominates the trade misinvoicing adjustments, overshadowing export under-invoicing and resulting in a lower capital flight estimate than the unadjusted residual measure. Finally, and somewhat surprisingly given the scale of its oil exports, Angola is a case where the misinvoicing adjustments are small relative to the overall magnitude of capital flight.

Remittance discrepancies Sizeable discrepancies exist for many African countries between workers' remittances estimated from survey data, as described above, and those recorded in the official balance-of-payments accounts. This reflects the fact that large volumes of remittances are transferred through informal channels, in part to avoid onerous fees charged on transfers through the formal banking system. In Nigeria, South Africa, Angola and Ghana – the four countries with the largest discrepancies – we estimate that unrecorded inflows in each case amounted to more than $10 billion (in 2008 dollars) over the 1970–2008 period. For the thirty-three countries together, we estimate the total at $125 billion.

Apart from their importance for accurate measurement of capital flight, remittances to African countries deserve serious attention in their own right. They represent an important source of private capital flows to Africa that can help fill resource gaps faced by many countries on the continent. The Ethiopian Central Bank reports, for example, that official annual remittances inflows from the diaspora are about $500 million, and estimates that informal flows are about the same amount.[19] For some countries, including Nigeria and Kenya, remittances have surpassed both development assistance and foreign direct investment as a source of foreign exchange.[20]

For African rural households, in particular, whose incomes are low and frequently uncertain, a steady inflow of remittances can help them to avoid deprivation. Indeed, even a small drop in income may jeopardize their ability to afford basic needs, including food.[21]

The volume of remittances to the continent is expected to increase in future years, given recent trends of emigration from the continent.[22] African emigrants include substantial numbers of highly skilled workers, who are able to command relatively high wages in their host countries. It is estimated, for example, that one third of Kenya's skilled professionals are working outside of the country, and that among Zimbabwean university graduates the figure is 70 to 90 per cent.[23] Given the prevailing pull and push factors, it is unlikely that these trends will be reversed any time soon.

Africa as a net creditor

It is now time to balance the books. How much net financial wealth does Africa have, given its external assets and liabilities? To answer this question, we compare external assets, as measured by the cumulative stock of capital flight, to external debt. The assets accumulated by means of capital flight are private, while the external debts are public liabilities owed to the creditors by the people of Africa through 'their' governments.

Not all of the capital that fled sub-Saharan Africa can be presumed to have been saved and invested so as to earn normal rates of return. As we have noted, some of the money was spent on consumption, and some savings may have earned sub-normal rates of return. Our measure of cumulative capital flight, including interest earnings, therefore does not exactly equal the external assets held by private Africans today. We nonetheless believe that a comparison between the stock of capital flight and the external debt can provide a reasonable indicator of Africa's net wealth.

By this measure, sub-Saharan Africa is a net creditor to the rest of the world by a substantial margin. The cumulative stock of capital flight from the thirty-three countries covered in this book stood at $944 billion in 2008, compared to external debts of $177 billion. By this measure, these countries had positive net external assets to the tune of $767 billion (see Table 2.2). In other words, the rest of the world owes more to these African countries than they owe to the rest of the world. This suggests that Africa could expunge its entire stock of foreign debt if it could recover only a fraction of the wealth held by Africans in foreign financial centres around the world.

Many millions of Africans are desperately poor. But the continent is rich. According to the *World Wealth Report*, the continent had roughly 100,000 high net worth individuals in 2008, twice as many as a decade before. Of these, about 1,800 were 'ultra-high net worth individuals', with at least $30 million each in investable assets.[24] Together these rich Africans held about $800 billion in investable assets in 2008.

Compared to other regions, African private wealth holders exhibit a stronger preference for foreign assets as opposed to domestic assets. According to a study by researchers at the World Bank and IMF, an astonishing 40 per cent of Africa's total private wealth was held abroad as flight capital in 1990. The corresponding figure for South Asia was 5 per cent. For East Asia it was 6 per cent, and for Latin America 10 per cent. Sub-Saharan Africa and South Asia had similar levels of total private wealth per worker, but in sub-Saharan Africa capital flight amounted to $696 per worker whereas in South Asia it was only $90 per worker. As a result, private domestic capital per worker in Africa was less than 60 per cent of what it was in South Asia.[25]

High net worth individuals typically have more internationally diversified portfolios than their poorer countrymen. According to the *World Wealth Report*, high net worth individuals in the Asia-Pacific region hold 32 per cent of their assets abroad and those in Latin America hold 55 per cent abroad, percentages roughly five times higher than the overall averages for these regions reported by the World Bank and the IMF.[26] If the same pattern holds in Africa, this would suggest that the greater part of the wealth of high net worth Africans is invested abroad. In this respect, the ultra-rich of Africa today are unlike the robber barons of years gone by in the industrialized countries, who whatever their misdeeds at least did invest in their nations' economies.

The preference for foreign assets and aversion to domestic investment comes at a high opportunity cost to African economies. In the case of legally acquired assets, the continent is deprived of the gains that would accrue from investment at home, not only losing income and jobs, but also forgoing government revenue that could fund public services. In the case of illegally acquired assets, African countries lose twice: first, they are robbed through fraud and embezzlement; then they are further deprived of any benefits that would trickle down if the loot were invested at home.

Bleeding a continent: the costs of capital flight ★

Africa is bleeding money, as capital flows into the private accounts of African elites and their accomplices in Western financial centres. At the same time, the continent is in dire need of financing. For Africa to overcome widespread and extreme poverty, it needs sustained and sustainable economic growth. This will require very large increases in the levels of domestic investment, especially in infrastructure.[27]

A continent in need of investment Researchers and development institutions have invested considerable time and energy to prove that African countries need more resources to meet their infrastructure financing needs. The 2009 Africa Infrastructure Country Diagnostic report concluded that Africa's middle-income countries need investment of about 10 per cent of GDP per year in infrastructure alone.[28] Investment needs for low-income African countries are higher at about 15 per cent of GDP annually. To achieve these levels, the continent's investment would need to be scaled up by at least $100 billion per year to nearly double the current level.

To get a first-hand sense of the immensity of the problem, one need only experience any of the cities in sub-Saharan Africa. In July 2009, one of the authors of this book, Léonce Ndikumana, visited

55

Freetown, the capital of Sierra Leone, to attend a meeting of the African Caucus of Finance Ministers and Central Bank Governors. Although this was his first trip to Sierra Leone, he did not expect any surprises; after all, he was going to an African country, and he had been in quite a number of them. But the visit to Freetown turned out to be an opportunity to experience something new: a city that is effectively cut off from its own airport. To get from the airport to the city, there are three options: a very long road trip around the bay that separates the two; a ferry that is subject to long waits and the risk of capsizing due to overloading; or a seven-minute ride in a helicopter, which is most convenient (for those who can afford it) but also risky, since these have been known to drop in bad weather with no survivors. On this occasion, the helicopter made the journey safely. The cost of building a bridge to link the city to the airport has been estimated at $400 million, a modest fraction of the $6 billion in capital flight that has left Sierra Leone since 1970.[29] Despite the economic benefits that such a bridge would bring to the country and the region, the government has not been able to mobilize the necessary money.

Sierra Leone is by no means alone in its dire lack of basic infrastructure. In fact, apart from the helicopter, Ndikumana's experience in Sierra Leone was little different from what he encounters in his native country, Burundi, when he visits his commune of Vugizo in the south. The commune has the agricultural potential to feed the towns and cities in the province and beyond, but it is landlocked and has poor access to markets. During the rainy season, it can take two hours to drive the 40-kilometre stretch of dirt track linking it to the nearest paved road.[30]

The Millennium Development Goal (MDG) of halving extreme poverty by 2015 remains elusive for much of Africa. The MDG Africa Steering Group estimated in 2008 that for Africa to achieve this and related development goals, public external financing would have to increase by $72 billion per year in the medium term.[31] Were Africa able to recoup only a fraction of what it has lost in capital flight, this would go a long way towards filling this gap.

The United Nations Economic Commission on Africa estimated in 1999 that an investment/GDP ratio of 34 per cent would be required to achieve a 7 per cent GDP growth rate in Africa, which would cut poverty by half by 2015.[32] This investment target is in reach for African countries if they can manage to stem capital flight and recoup some of the money stolen in the past.[33] Otherwise, efforts to mobilize additional development financing for growth and poverty reduction will yield only limited results.

Capital flight and tax revenue Sub-Saharan African governments badly need tax revenue to bridge the large deficits in the provision of public goods, including not only infrastructure but also health and education.[34] Some resource-rich countries have seen revenue gains thanks to natural resource booms, but these may prove to be transient. Meanwhile, very few non-resource-rich African countries have recorded sustained increases in revenue.[35]

Countries with higher capital flight tend to have lower tax revenue, as can be seen in Figure 2.3. There are two reasons for this negative relationship. First, capital flight directly erodes the

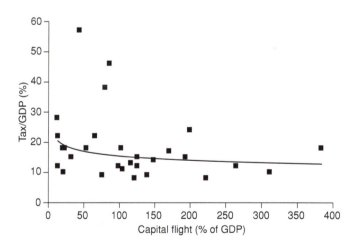

2.3 Capital flight and tax revenue *Sources*: Tax/GDP ratio: average for the years 2006–08 from World Bank, World Development Indicators, and IMF country information. Capital flight: cumulative real capital flight, 1970–2008, from Appendix Table A.2.

tax base by subtracting from it private wealth and income earnings on that wealth. Second, high capital flight is symptomatic of an environment characterized by corruption and weak regulation, circumstances that both promote capital flight and undermine tax administration. (In contrast, if capital flight were motivated primarily by a desire to escape high taxes, one would expect the opposite correlation: countries with less tax revenue would tend to have less capital flight.)

If we look at the 'tax effort' – the ratio of the actual tax revenue to the potential revenue based on the country's economic structure and level of development – we find that actual tax performance in sub-Saharan Africa generally remains well below potential, and that resource-rich countries tend to perform even worse in this respect than resource-scarce countries.[36] In the case of Nigeria, for example, when oil rents are excluded, the tax effort index is 0.44, meaning that the country is generating only 44 per cent of its potential tax revenue from non-oil sectors. In Angola, the corresponding index is 0.39. Natural resource revenues are often poorly mobilized, too. In the Democratic Republic of Congo, for example, it is reported that gold exports can reach up to one billion dollars a year, but these exports generate a negligible $37,000 in tax revenue.[37]

Rampant tax exemptions contribute to low revenues. Often exemptions are awarded not on the basis of the criteria set by the law – which typically aim to stimulate private economic activity, for example by means of tax incentives – but rather on the basis of the political influence of individuals and firms. As a result, tax revenue may not follow the expansion of private sector activity and private wealth. A case study on Ethiopia, where resource inflows to the private sector are increasing but the proceeds from corporate taxation are declining, estimates that the revenue forgone through exemptions doubled between 2005 and 2007.[38] At the same time, Ethiopia has a relatively high nominal income tax rate, which may contribute to greater tax fraud. Taxes that are high in theory thus can be low in practice, owing to both legal exemptions and illegal evasion.

Capital flight has substantial adverse distributional effects, too, exacerbating gaps between rich and poor. The rich, by virtue of the fact that they hold a larger share of their assets abroad, are shielded from the wealth effects of devaluation of the national currency. Indeed, they may benefit from devaluation, as this allows them to reap windfall gains if they bring some of their capital back into the country. Since capital flight itself puts pressure on the exchange rate, it increases the likelihood of this exchange-rate effect.

At the same time, by depressing government tax revenue, capital flight adversely affects the poorer segments of the population who depend most heavily on publicly funded services. For example, when the government is unable to provide adequate medical supplies and qualified health personnel for public hospitals, the poor who cannot afford the alternative of going to private clinics suffer the most. The same goes for education. We will return to this point in Chapter 4.

3 | The revolving door

At first blush it may seem paradoxical that foreign lenders sent billions of dollars to African governments at the same time as private Africans were sending billions out as capital flight. In a simple textbook world, both would respond similarly to local economic conditions. If the investment climate is favourable, foreign dollars flow in and local dollars stay at home. If it is not, foreign lending dries up and local capital departs in search of higher returns.

Once we move beyond textbook economics to real-world economies, the paradox begins to lift. In the real world, not all capital is acquired by honest means – some is accumulated through fraud, kickbacks, padded contracts, bribery and outright theft. And in the real world, not all movements of capital across international borders are declared to monetary authorities – some moves via trade misinvoicing, clandestine wire transfers and suitcases of smuggled cash. This is why the balance-of-payments accounts typically do not, in fact, balance, as discussed in Chapter 2, and it is what enables us to calculate capital flight as the missing-money residual.

These two phenomena – the illicit acquisition of capital and the illicit movement of capital – are interconnected. Individuals who obtain wealth by questionable means are not inclined to leave their money in plain sight where it may attract inconvenient scrutiny. They are unlikely to be scrupulous about paying taxes on this wealth and any earnings it generates. And they generally find it prudent to ship a substantial fraction of the loot out of the country to 'safe havens' that are insulated from unwelcome changes in the political climate at home.

Foreign loans can be an important source of illicit wealth, and hence of capital flight, for reasons explored in Chapter 1.

On both sides of international lending agreements there are perverse incentives: borrowers who contract liabilities in the name of the public with the aim of siphoning funds into private assets, and creditors driven by the imperative to 'move the money' and comforted by the prospect of bailouts when their loans go sour. The result can be a revolving door, in which money flows in from foreign lenders and flows back out as capital flight.

How widespread is this phenomenon? In this chapter we investigate the extent to which capital flight from sub-Saharan Africa has been fuelled by foreign borrowing. We do this by examining the statistical relationship between the two.

Debt-fuelled capital flight

Capital flight can be linked to foreign borrowing in four ways. These are depicted in Table 3.1. The tightest linkages occur when one directly fuels the other: that is, when the same money flows in and out through the revolving door. In the case of *debt-fuelled capital flight*, our primary concern in this book, loans from foreign creditors to African governments finance the accumulation of private wealth via the illicit mechanisms described in Chapter 1: the diversion of funds from public accounts into private accounts, kickbacks (or more politely, commissions) on government contracts, inflated procurement costs, ghost projects, and so on. The beneficiaries of these loan-siphoning arrangements then park part or all of the proceeds in safe havens abroad.

TABLE 3.1 Linkages between foreign borrowing and capital flight

	Debt → Capital flight	Capital flight → Debt
Motive and means	Debt-fuelled capital flight	Flight-fuelled foreign borrowing
Motive only	Debt-driven capital flight	Flight-driven foreign borrowing

In the case of *flight-fuelled foreign borrowing*, a similar direct link operates in the reverse direction: private wealth holders first move funds into an offshore bank account, and then they 'borrow' back the money from the same bank, a phenomenon known as 'round-tripping' or a 'back-to-back loan'. This technique was pioneered by the American organized crime financier Meyer Lansky in the 1930s as a way to launder money in Switzerland, the aim being to conceal the origins of the funds in question from suspicious government authorities. Lansky's clients reaped a fringe benefit, too: interest payments on these pseudo-loans were tax-deductible.[1] In developing countries today, where foreign loans to private borrowers generally come with an explicit or implicit guarantee that the government will assume the liability should the borrower default, a further attraction to the round-tripper is the prospect of shifting the resulting debt on to the government. In most of sub-Saharan Africa, foreign loans to private borrowers (even with public guarantees) have been relatively rare, so this phenomenon is likely to have been less widespread than in many Asian and Latin American countries.

In addition to these direct linkages, there are more indirect ones, again running in both directions. In the case of *debt-driven capital flight*, foreign borrowing provides a motive for capital flight but not the actual money. The motive comes from the actual and anticipated economic impacts of the debt. In the short run, the influx of borrowed money pushes up the value of the domestic currency. But over the long run, as the stock of debt grows, so does the prospect that the net transfer will turn negative, leading to eventual depreciation of the domestic currency. By moving capital into hard currency accounts offshore while the value of the local currency is artificially inflated, the flight capitalist not only insures against this exchange-rate risk but also stands to reap a profit in the event of devaluation. Similarly, a large and growing debt overhang may raise fears among the wealthy that increased taxes or other regulations will reduce the value of assets held domestically, motivating them to send money abroad.

Finally, in the case of *flight-driven foreign borrowing*, capital flight generates demand for replacement funds that are borrowed from foreign lenders. On the borrower side, as the tax base is

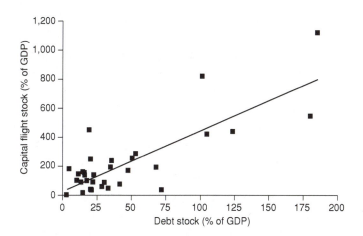

3.1 Cumulative capital flight and external debt, 1970–2008 *Sources*: Capital flight stock (with imputed interest earnings) from Table A.2; external debt and GDP (2008) from World Bank, Global Development Finance database.

sapped by capital flight, African governments may seek foreign loans to finance expenditures. On the creditor side, the short-run incentives for loan-pushing, described in Chapter 1, coupled with the long-run expectation of bailouts, explain why lenders are willing to lend money even as private Africans move money in the opposite direction.

Insofar as these linkages are in operation, we expect to find a positive correlation between capital flight and foreign debt – the precise opposite of what we might expect in the simplified world of textbook economics, where all capital movements are legitimate and all economic actors, whether official creditors, commercial banks or high net worth Africans, respond to similar incentives in deciding where to put their money.

Figure 3.1 shows the correlation across African countries between the cumulative stock of 1970–2008 capital flight and the stock of external debt in 2008, with both expressed as percentages of GDP to control for differences in the size of the different countries' economies. This picture is consistent with the proposition that capital flight and external debt are indeed intertwined.[2]

Three

How much money spins through the revolving door? A key difference between the direct and indirect effects of foreign borrowing on capital flight lies in the timing of these effects. In the case of debt-fuelled capital flight (and its cousin, flight-fuelled foreign borrowing), the revolving door spins quickly, and we can expect to find a strong year-to-year correlation between inflows of foreign borrowing and outflows of capital flight. In the case of debt-driven capital flight (and its cousin, flight-driven foreign borrowing), by contrast, the relationship is cumulative: it is the total stocks of external debt and capital flight which drive each other, so there is no compelling reason to expect tight year-to-year correlations between annual flows in both directions. Assume, for example, that an African country adds to its debt stock in a given year, but that it borrows less than it did in the previous year. We expect debt-fuelled capital flight to decrease, too, as there is less money coming through the revolving door. But we expect debt-driven capital flight to increase, as the debt overhang grows.

This difference makes it possible to use statistical tools to distinguish between direct and indirect linkages and to estimate their respective magnitudes. In econometric studies published in the professional journals *World Development* and the *International Review of Applied Economics*, we have estimated the magnitude and statistical significance of both sorts of effects in sub-Saharan Africa.[3] First, we investigated the effects of current borrowing – that is, annual inflows that add to the country's total stock of external debt – on year-to-year variations in capital flight. Secondly, we investigated the effects of the total debt stock on capital flight.

The results suggest that foreign loans have indeed fuelled capital flight in the short run, and that the accumulated stock of debt drives additional capital flight in the long run. We find that for every dollar of foreign loans to sub-Saharan Africa, *roughly 60 cents flow back out as capital flight in the same year.* In other words, we find statistical evidence of debt-fuelled capital flight on a large scale. We also find that every one-dollar increase in the stock of external debt is associated with 2–4 cents of additional capital flight annually *in subsequent years.* In other words, we find statistical evidence that debt-driven capital flight is a significant drain on African economies as well.

As a further statistical test of these relationships between capital flight and external borrowing, we carried out the same exercise using a different proxy measure of private wealth held abroad by Africans: the deposits held by African individuals and firms in Western banks (formally, these are called 'external positions of reporting banks vis-à-vis the non-bank sector').[4] These officially recorded holdings in Western banks represent only a fraction of African capital flight. They omit non-bank financial assets such as stocks and bonds, real estate and other non-financial property, holdings in non-Western banks, and Western bank accounts in which the African identity of the depositor is concealed, as well as capital flight that was used to finance overseas consumption rather than being saved. For all these reasons, the proxy measure is much smaller than our measure of total capital flight. For the thirty-three African countries in our study, recorded bank deposits in 2008 amounted to $42.1 billion, or 5.7 per cent of cumulative real capital flight in the 1970–2008 period (reported in Table A.2).[5]

Using this proxy measure, we again found that both annual inflows of foreign loans and the total stock of external debt have positive and statistically significant effects on capital flight. As expected, the estimated magnitude of the effects is smaller: one dollar of new borrowing is associated with between 2 and 17 cents of deposits by Africans in foreign banks in the same year, and with about one extra cent of additional deposits annually in subsequent years. The positive relationship between capital flight and external borrowing is thus evident even when we use this quite restrictive proxy measure for capital flight.

Capital flight as portfolio choice? Not all capital that flees Africa was illicitly acquired. Some capital flight involves outflows of honestly acquired assets. In textbook economics, such capital movements are attributed to portfolio choices by investors seeking to maximize risk-adjusted returns to capital.[6] The rates of return are expected to equalize across countries and markets, assuming that economic agents have access to complete information and that transactions costs are negligible. In such a world, systematic capital outflows from Africa would imply that returns to capital are systematically higher abroad.

To assess the extent to which Africans hold funds abroad as a result of relative rate-of-return considerations, we examined the statistical relationship between capital flight and the difference in interest rates, adjusted for inflation, between African countries and the rest of the world. Using the short-term US Treasury bill rate as a proxy for the world interest rate, we found no statistically significant effect of the interest rate differential on capital flight.[7] We conclude, therefore, that African capital flight cannot be explained adequately by conventional portfolio choice theory.

Moreover, if the rate of return to capital is lower in African countries than in the industrialized countries – or if investment is riskier in Africa, so that risk-adjusted returns are lower – this should discourage foreign lenders as well as domestic investors. As economist Manuel Pastor puts it, 'If the investment climate in a country is negative enough to push out local capital, why would savvy international bankers extend their own capital in the form of loans?'[8]

This paradox points to the existence of what economists call 'asymmetric risk'.[9] Domestic capital may face a greater risk of seizure, particularly if it has been obtained by questionable means and if political circumstances change so as to reduce the owner's degree of protection. Meanwhile, foreign capital may be guaranteed against this risk by the government or by international institutions.[10] Under these circumstances, private Africans may find it in their interest to invest abroad, even as foreign creditors find it profitable to issue loans to African governments. When the meaning of 'portfolio choice' is expanded to encompass these very different motives for borrowing and investing, we can reconcile the phenomena of simultaneous foreign borrowing and capital flight.

Foreign aid: less likely to fuel capital flight? In addition to loans, African countries also receive external funding in the form of grants from aid donors. In fact, for low-income African countries, grants and official loans with a high 'grant element' (by virtue of below-market interest rates) make up the bulk of their external financing. African countries have experienced capital flight even as they received substantial amounts of foreign aid.[11] It is therefore natural to ask whether the two are related.

In a multi-country study of the effects of official development aid on capital flight, economists Paul Collier, Anke Hoeffler and Catherine Pattillo found that at low levels, aid tends to deter capital flight, but that at high levels, aid tends to induce greater capital flight.[12] They calculate that the turning point at which the inducement effect starts to dominate the deterrent effect is beyond the observed aid levels for most of the African countries in their sample, implying that aid to Africa is not associated with more capital flight.

Yet aid is a lootable resource, much like other forms of public external borrowing. Donors cannot fully monitor its use, either because it is practically difficult or because they do not wish to put pressure on a particular government for political reasons. As a result, corrupt government officials and their cronies can and sometimes do embezzle aid and channel the funds abroad. Zaire under Mobutu is a case in point.[13] Given the substantial share of official loans in the debts of African countries, our results do not support the view that aid has been immune from the operation of the revolving door.

We also find that capital flight tends to be like bad grass in the field: once it has become rooted, it is hard to get rid of it. Our statistical studies show that countries that have experienced high levels of capital flight in the past tend to experience higher capital flight in subsequent years. This suggests that capital flight may be habit-forming, making it unlikely that any improvements in the investment climate will lead to its rapid disappearance.

The greasy spigot: oil and capital flight

Revenues from the extraction of natural resources can also serve as fuel for capital flight. These revenues come in three main forms: first, as 'signature bonuses', one-time payments by multinational enterprises in return for development rights; secondly, as royalties or taxes on oil and mineral exports; and thirdly, as resource-backed loans, such as the oil-backed loans described in Chapter 1.

The Angolan government, for example, is reported to have received $879 million in signature bonuses from oil companies in the year 1999 alone; about $3 billion per year in oil taxes in 2000 and 2001; and about $3.5 billion in oil-backed loans over the same two years.[14] The oil-backed loans from private creditors allowed the government to circumvent the efforts of the World Bank and the IMF to make further lending conditional on greater accountability and transparency in revenue management.[15] To this end, the state oil company Sonangol set up offshore accounts into which income from Angolan oil exports was deposited; the oil-backed loans were repaid directly from these accounts, entirely bypassing the country's domestic financial system.[16] 'Because of high interest rates, typically 2 percentage points above Libor [the London inter-bank offer rate], and safe repayment structures,' the *Financial Times* reported, 'the banks' appetites for these oil-backed loans are voracious.'[17]

Oil revenues allowed senior Angolan leaders to amass vast personal assets overseas. A 2002 IMF report, leaked to the press after its publication was blocked by the Angolan government, found that more than $900 million in oil revenues had gone missing from state coffers in 2001 – roughly three times the total value of humanitarian aid to Angola – and that $4 billion had disappeared in the previous five years.[18] In the same year, the non-governmental organization Global Witness traced $1.1 billion from Angolan oil revenues to a single bank account in the British Virgin Islands.[19]

To investigate the role of oil's greasy spigot in African capital flight, we compiled country-specific data on annual oil exports and added this to our statistical analysis of the determinants of the magnitude of capital flight. The relationship is positive and statistically significant: for each extra dollar in oil exports, we estimate that an additional 11 to 26 cents leave the country as capital flight.[20] This comes on top of the capital flight fuelled by foreign borrowing, including oil-backed loans.

We also examined the impact of non-oil mineral exports. In this case, we do not find a statistically significant relationship. Why the difference? The countries in our sample that are rich in mineral resources, but not oil, are a diverse group that includes Botswana, South Africa, Mozambique, Zambia, Ghana and Guinea. Several of these countries have relatively strong records in terms of both economic growth and revenue mobilization, compared to oil-rich countries like Nigeria, Angola and the Republic of Congo.[21] We suspect that the difference can be traced more to the institutional characteristics of these countries than to intrinsic characteristics of the resources themselves. In other words, there may be no inherent reason to expect that oil revenues are necessarily more prone to capital flight than other mineral revenues.

In theory, and sometimes perhaps in practice, resource-backed loans can be an effective vehicle to finance bona fide development rather than capital flight. China, which recently overtook Japan as the world's second-largest economy, benefited from this type of finance from the same economic superpower it has now surpassed: three decades ago the Chinese government obtained more than $10 billion in Japanese loans to fund construction of railways, ports and electrical power infrastructure, agreeing to repay the loans with shipments of oil, coal and minerals.[22]

Today China is entering into similar arrangements with a number of African countries. As of 2004, China became Africa's second-leading trade partner after the European Union.[23] Since then, China has provided about $14 billion in resource-backed infrastructure loans to African countries, including an oil-backed loan to the Republic of Congo, a loan to the Democratic Republic of Congo (DRC) to be repaid with exports of copper and cobalt, and a loan to Ghana to be repaid in shipments of cocoa beans.[24]

An attractive feature of these loans is that the infrastructure investments, built by a combination of Chinese and African labour, provide a tangible counterpart to the resources being extracted from Africa. In exchange for the copper and cobalt, for example, the DRC gets railways, roads and other public goods. For ordinary Congolese people, the near-barter-trade arrangement means that they can see, feel and touch the proceeds of the transaction. They may regard this as a better deal than what they had under colonial rule, when Belgium got the Congo's resources and all the country had to show for the digging of its precious metals was mounds of dirt. It also looks good compared to oil-backed loans from Western bankers to African governments, the counterparts of which are cash in secret offshore accounts or guns to suppress the regime's opponents.

Another attraction of the resource-backed loans is that they allow African countries to access finance that otherwise would not be available. For African countries classified as low-income countries (LICs), market loans are typically out of reach, and their ability to access concessional loans from official creditors is constrained by quotas and by conditionalities that penalize countries with poor 'institutional performance'.[25] These LICs can become trapped in a vicious circle of low institutional capacity, financing constraints and low capacity to improve their institutions. Resource-backed loans may offer one way out of this impasse.

These loans are not immune to pathologies that have plagued other foreign loans to African governments, however. A National Assembly inquiry in the DRC reported in 2010 that more than $23 million in signature bonuses on the copper-backed loan had been stolen.[26] And there is concern, particularly among Western governments, that the Chinese loans will support corrupt and authoritarian regimes. But as Deborah Brautigam, author of *The Dragon's Gift*, a study of Chinese investment in Africa, points out, 'the West also supports such regimes when it advances its interests'.[27]

Other creditors are getting into the business of resource-backed lending to Africa, too. For example, shortly after China's Export-Import Bank extended $2 billion in credit to Angola in 2004, Standard Chartered Bank followed with another $2.25 billion oil-backed loan, drawing criticisms from civil society groups for the lack of transparency surrounding the deal.[28] In addition to China, other 'emerging partners' are lining up to enter this sector. Thus India and Brazil have signed or announced oil-for-infrastructure loans in several African countries.[29] From the perspective of economic development, this growing trend raises the question of whether African countries are ready to engage in a way that maximizes their share of the income from natural resource endowments and puts this income to productive use. The partners certainly have a strategy of engagement with Africa. The question is: does Africa have one, too?[30]

Foreign loans: the good, the bad and the capital-starved

Before concluding this chapter, we want to make it clear what our analysis is and is not saying about foreign loans. The evidence presented in this chapter has demonstrated that there is a strong link between external financing and capital flight via the phenomenon of debt-fuelled capital flight. The evidence indicates that a substantial fraction of the funds that African governments have secured from lending institutions and development partners either never made it to Africa or were diverted into the private pockets of politically influential individuals and their associates. For this reason, a substantial fraction of Africa's debt can be considered 'odious', in that the people of Africa have no moral or legal obligation to repay loans that did not serve bona fide purposes. We return to this issue in the final chapter of the book.

Our analysis does not suggest, however, that all loans go into capital flight or that all debt is odious. Africa's landscape is certainly replete with examples of inefficient use of foreign loans; African fields count plenty of (dead) 'white elephants', and as we have seen, much of the borrowed money came to rest outside of Africa. At the same time, many good things have happened on the continent thanks to aid and external borrowing. Roads have been built, linking markets and reducing the cost of doing business. Children have been educated, clinics have been constructed in rural areas, and mosquito nets have been distributed in malaria-infested areas, all with external support.

Ample testimonies as to the benefits of aid, including official lending, can be found in various areas, especially in health and education. For children born in low-income households in Africa, aid allows them to attend school, and allows some of them to move up the social ladder to become national leaders and even to reach the global stage. An example can be found right here in this book – one of the authors, Léonce Ndikumana, is a product of donor-funded public education from high school all the way to graduate school. The story began in 1972, as Burundi was experiencing a wave of bloody ethnic violence that took the life of his father. Having just completed elementary school in Martyazo in southern Burundi, Léonce was one of seven students from his school who were selected to attend the Ecole Normale de Rutovu, a high school sponsored by Canadian Catholic brothers. The opportunity to attend high school in Rutovu marked the beginning of a successful educational experience that would eventually lead Léonce to the University of Burundi and then to Washington University in St Louis in the United States. The economics department at the University of Burundi at that time, along with the science departments and the medical school, was well equipped thanks to grants from bilateral aid donors. Léonce's graduate school was also funded by a grant from the US Agency for International Development. Similar stories can be told of the majority of Burundian intellectuals, most of whom come from modest upbringings and would not have been able to afford higher education. It is also the story of many Africans in other countries whose upward social mobility was made possible by aid to education. Foreign loans and aid are valuable to the extent that they are put to good use.

In principle, and at times in practice, foreign loans and grants can help African countries implement national development plans by filling the gap between domestic revenue and the costs of development projects. For example, in 2009, when Botswana faced a financing shortfall due to declining export revenues in the wake of the global economic crisis, the government approached the African Development Bank for the first time to request a $1.5 billion budget-support loan. This loan allowed the government to meet its recurrent expenses and to finance planned infrastructure projects that otherwise would have had to be postponed.

Yet without the right incentives and good management, loans can and often do yield bad results, as we have seen, funding wasteful expenditures and financing private wealth accumulation. For this reason, some analysts and donors have taken the view that development assistance should be universally preconditioned on 'good governance'. This solution poses a quandary in countries with weak governance institutions, including countries coming out of civil wars or at risk of violent conflict. In these settings, inadequate aid can exacerbate hardship and societal tensions, but misguided or misused aid can exacerbate these, too. Aid can yield positive results if it helps to build effective and sustainable institutions.[31]

In the majority of African countries, aid currently is not enough to meet the massive investment needs. It is difficult to achieve meaningful development results if aid only trickles in small and unpredictable amounts. Low-income African countries, in particular, find themselves in a problematic situation: they receive inadequate aid and at the same time conditionalities imposed by the international financial institutions impede their access to private capital markets to raise additional funds. Yet some of these countries are now demonstrating the capacity to raise substantial amounts of financing from domestic and international bond markets. Ghana recently raised $750 million through Eurobond issues to finance infrastructure. Similarly, the Kenyan government's domestic-currency infrastructure bond issue was oversubscribed by a large margin. There are clear needs for development financing across Africa today.

The choices are not (or need not be) simply between bad loans or no loans. Good loans are possible, too. But making this possibility a reality will require systemic reforms in lending practices by financial institutions, and in the management and use of external resources by African governments. The solution is not to 'pull the plug' on African countries, but to plug the leaks and fix the perverse incentives that have sapped the effectiveness of loans and aid in the past.

4 | The human costs

Capital flight drains resources from Africa. So does debt service on loans that financed capital flight. The human costs of this drain can be glimpsed at the Centre Hospitalier Universitaire de Brazzaville, the main hospital in the Republic of Congo, where patients are carried up and down the stairwells on people's backs because broken lifts have not been repaired. A French researcher grimly observes, 'Only the morgue operates at full tilt.'[1]

In 2005 Congo's government spent $101 million on external debt service – more than it spent on public health. The Republic of Congo is one of five African countries where child mortality increased between 1990 and 2008.[2] Only 6 per cent of children sleep under mosquito nets that protect against malaria, the disease that accounts for one in five of all childhood deaths in Africa.[3]

Congo is not alone. Across sub-Saharan Africa, many governments today spend more on debt service than on health for their people.

Africa's quiet violence

In the decades since independence, violent conflicts have taken the lives of many Africans. Between 1960 and 2005, Africa experienced about 1.6 million battle deaths.[4] The toll is multiplied by deaths due to war-related disease and starvation and the breakdown of healthcare systems. For example, including deaths from these causes, the war in the Democratic Republic of Congo claimed an estimated 5.4 million lives from 1998 to 2008, making it the world's deadliest conflict since the Second World War.[5]

In recent years, the number of violent conflicts in Africa and the associated death toll have subsided. We can hope that this trend will continue in the future, and that war will recede as a cause of human suffering and death.

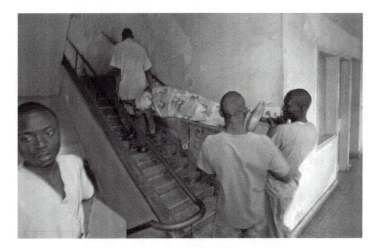

5 'The main teaching hospital here is in such disrepair that many patients have to pay freelance porters for piggyback rides up and down the stairs to get X-rays. It costs $2 a flight, each way,' the *New York Times* reported from Brazzaville in December 2007 (*New York Times*)

But the continent continues to wage an equally devastating battle against the quiet violence of needless disease and hunger. The majority of deaths in Africa are caused by diseases that are preventable and curable with existing medicines and technology.

Each year, for example, nearly one million children under the age of five die from malaria worldwide. About 75 per cent of them are Africans.[6] Diarrhoea and pneumonia, both curable diseases, together account for 35 per cent of Africa's child deaths.

Apart from the human cost, the economic impacts of these diseases are also large. It has been estimated, for example, that Africa loses more than $12 billion of GDP every year owing to malaria.[7]

Why? Malaria has been virtually eradicated in many places in the world. Premature death rates from other diseases have been greatly reduced elsewhere. But in Africa programmes for prevention and cure either do not exist or are inadequately funded.

It may be true, as economist Jeffrey Sachs has remarked, that Africa is 'really unlucky when it comes to malaria: high temperatures, plenty of breeding sites, and mosquitoes that prefer humans to cattle'.[8] But the real cause of the failure to conquer malaria in Africa is not bad luck; it is insufficient funding for prevention and treatment. Fewer than one in five African children sleep under mosquito-proofed nets. Until recently, as Sachs notes, malaria rarely figured on the agenda of Africa's international aid partners: 'Malaria was not on the policy radar screen. The IMF and World Bank were apparently too busy arguing for budget cuts and privatization of sugar mills to have much left to deal with malaria.'[9]

In addition to inadequate international funding, national resources are poorly managed. The problem is particularly striking in the case of resource-rich countries. In Equatorial Guinea, for example, the low coverage of anti-malaria programmes contributes to high mortality rates, especially among children. Malaria mortality in Equatorial Guinea is more than twice the African average.[10] While the people battle disease, the country's elite squanders the nation's oil wealth on personal luxuries. Teodorin

Obiang, the president's son, is reported to have a $35 million mansion in Malibu, California, as well as multiple foreign bank accounts.[11] In 2011 Global Witness reported that he had commissioned plans for a 118-metre 'superyacht' complete with its own cinema, restaurant, bar and swimming pool. The yacht's price tag would be $380 million, three times Equatorial Guinea's annual budget for health and education combined.[12]

In a similar vein, Global Witness reports that one month of private spending by Denis Christel Sassou Nguesso, the son of the Republic of Congo's president, could have paid for vaccinations against measles for more than 80,000 Congolese babies.[13] Measles is a leading cause of child deaths in his country.

Water-borne diseases are a major cause of ill health and deaths in Africa, especially among children. This is a result of lack of access to clean drinking water and sanitation facilities. In Nigeria, for example, only 58 per cent of the population has access to clean drinking water sources, despite the country's oil wealth.[14] Only 34 per cent of Africa's population had access to sanitation facilities in 2008, only a slight improvement on 30 per cent in 1990. In Latin America, by contrast, the corresponding figure is 87 per cent.

As a result of inadequate funding from both national and international sources, Africa has too few health facilities, and those that exist do not have adequate equipment or personnel. Africa on average has only eleven nurses and midwives per 10,000 inhabitants, less than half the world average of twenty-eight.[15]

Access to the services and facilities that do exist is grossly unequal. Rural households often live far from health facilities, and the poor in general are at a disadvantage since they cannot afford to pay for private healthcare. In Côte d'Ivoire, for example, among the richest fifth of families, 95 per cent of childbirths are attended by skilled health staff; among the poorest fifth the figure is less than 30 per cent. In Nigeria, the corresponding ratios are 86 per cent for the top fifth of households, and only 8 per cent for the poorest fifth.[16]

Every year millions of children worldwide die before reaching their fifth birthday. UNICEF reports that 'malnutrition is a contributing factor in more than half these young deaths', and that more than half die at home owing to lack of access to health facilities.[17] Thanks to medical progress, child mortality worldwide has declined by more than a half in the past five decades, from 20 million deaths in 1960 to 8.8 million in 2008. But progress has been very slow in sub-Saharan Africa, which has the highest child death rates.[18] In 2008, the continent lost 86 babies for every 1,000 births (see Table 4.1).

TABLE 4.1 Infant mortality (deaths per 1,000 live births)

Region	1980	2008	% change 1980–2008
Sub-Saharan Africa	115	86	−25.2
South Asia	114	58	−49.1
Middle East & North Africa	94	29	−69.2
East Asia & Pacific	54	23	−57.4
Latin America & Caribbean	63	20	−69.2
Eastern Europe & Central Asia	53	19	−64.1
High-income (OECD)	12	5	−58.3

Source: World Bank, World Development Indicators database

The 2010 Millennium Development Goals (MDG) Global Monitoring Report observes, 'Sub-Saharan Africa has 20 percent of the world's children under age five, but 50 percent of all child deaths.'[19] Only Seychelles and Cape Verde have reached the MDG target of 45 deaths per 1,000 children, and only a handful of African countries are expected to reduce child mortality to this level by 2015.

Historical evidence demonstrates that while growth in income helps to improve health outcomes, income alone is not enough.[20] Major public initiatives, such as water purification and supply, installation of sanitation systems, the draining of swamps, and mass vaccination campaigns, historically have played a key role in progress in health. For example, it is estimated that as much as half of the reduction in mortality in the first third of the twentieth century in the United States was a result of water purification alone.[21] This underscores the importance of public health expenditure in Africa.

On average, sub-Saharan African governments are currently spending $25 per person annually on healthcare (Table 4.2). This is less than half the amount spent in the Middle East and North Africa, and less than 1 per cent of public healthcare expenditure per person in the OECD countries. In some African countries per capita public spending on health care is in the single digits: at the bottom are Guinea at $2/year, Sierra Leone at $4/year and Ethiopia at $5/year (see Appendix Table A3).

TABLE 4.2 Public health expenditure (annual average, 2005–07)

Region	Public health expenditure	
	US$ per person	Share of GDP (%)
Sub-Saharan Africa	25.6	2.7
South Asia	8.5	1.1
East Asia & Pacific	36.0	1.8
Middle East & North Africa	64.8	2.8
Latin America & Caribbean	186.9	3.3
Eastern Europe & Central Asia	207.6	3.6
High-income (OECD)	2602.2	7.0

Source: World Bank, World Development Indicators database

In 2008 the MDG Africa Steering Group estimated that the continent needed an additional $10 billion per year by 2010 to improve health systems and reach the MDG targets in child mortality and maternal health. Another $17 billion per year was needed to finance programmes in Africa for the control of the major killer diseases.[22] In 2007 total international aid to the health sector in Africa amounted to $3.4 billion.[23]

In Figure 4.1 we show the relationship between public health expenditure and infant mortality for the thirty-three countries in our study in the period 2005–07. Statistical analysis indicates that

79

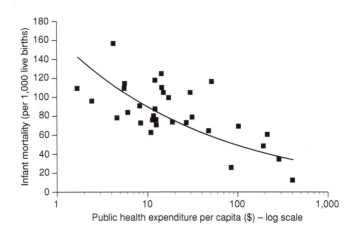

4.1 Infant mortality and public health expenditure, 2005–07
Source: Authors' calculations using data from the World Bank's
World Development Indicators database

one infant's life is saved for every $40,000 in extra spending on public health.[24] One million dollars in additional public health expenditure in sub-Saharan Africa thus translates into twenty-five fewer infant deaths.

When debt service is bad for your health

Many African countries devote a significant share of their scarce public revenues to paying external debt service. Much of the debt being serviced was used to finance capital flight, as we saw in the last chapter.

Debt service payments represent the third and final act in the tragedy of debt-fuelled capital flight. In the first two acts – foreign borrowing in the name of the public, and diversion of part or all of the money into private assets abroad – there is no net loss of capital from Africa. What comes in simply goes back out again. It is when African countries start to repay these debts that the resource drain begins.

Sub-Saharan African governments as a whole today are spending roughly the same amount on debt service as they spend on public health (see Table A3 in the appendix). In other words, if all the subcontinent's external debts were cancelled, and all the saved money allocated to healthcare, this would double health spending. The result undoubtedly would be greatly improved health outcomes for the African population in general and for the poor in particular.

In practice, of course, there is not a simple one-to-one relationship between debt service and public health spending. Healthcare is only one among many possible alternative uses for the money currently spent to repay foreign debts. To gauge the extent to which debt service payments actually are associated with less public health spending, we need to examine the behaviour of African governments, or what economists would call the 'revealed preferences' of fiscal policy-makers.

Total debt service payments from the thirty-three countries in our capital flight analysis averaged $19.2 billion in the years 2005–07. Figure 4.2 depicts the relationship between each country's debt service and public health expenditures in these years. Examining the correlation between the two, we find that each additional dollar paid in debt service is associated with 29 cents

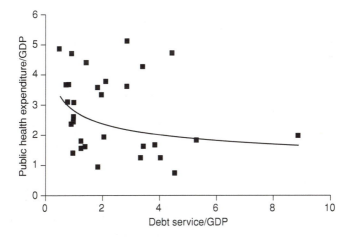

4.2 Public health expenditure and debt service (percentages of GDP, 2005–07) *Source*: Authors' calculations using data from the World Bank's World Development Indicators database

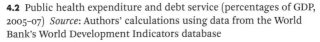

less spent on public health.[25] We estimate therefore that public health expenditures in these countries as a whole would have been $5.6 billion higher in the absence of debt-service payments.

The high levels of deaths in Africa from preventable and curable diseases are largely a result of lack of resources. These are in short supply, much below the needs. Moreover, the limited resources that exist are poorly managed and unequally distributed, compounding the problem. But when resources for healthcare are scaled up and well managed, the gains can be impressive. Several African countries, including Ethiopia, Rwanda, Tanzania and Zambia, have reduced malaria by as much as 50 per cent, for example, simply by distributing mosquito nets.[26]

Efforts to secure more funding for public health in Africa will require a multi-pronged approach. Internally, it will require mobilizing more domestic resources and increasing budgetary allocations to health systems. Externally, it will require raising more aid explicitly targeted at projects and activities that improve healthcare. It also will require curbing capital flight, launching strategies to recover Africa's stolen wealth, and staunching the ongoing drain of financial resources through debt service. The importance of the latter measures is clear when we make the connections between capital flight, debt service and health outcomes.

Connecting the dots

As we have documented in this chapter, debt-service payments force African governments to reduce public health expenditures. We estimate that one more dollar spent on debt service means 29 fewer cents spent on health. Less public health expenditure means that fewer clinics are built, less medicine is available in hospitals and pharmacies, and fewer healthcare workers can be employed.

To illustrate the human cost, we examined the correlation between public health expenditure and infant mortality. We found that each additional $40,000 of health spending is associated with one less infant death.

Putting these results together, we can calculate the impact

of debt service on infant mortality. A million-dollar increase in debt service reduces government health expenditures by about $290,000. This translates into seven more infant deaths. For every $140,000 that sub-Saharan Africa pays in external debt service, another African baby dies.

This is a conservative estimate of the human costs of debt service. It omits other impacts of lower public health expenditure: higher mortality among children aged one to five (infant mortality refers only to the first year of life), higher premature deaths of older children and adults, and effects of non-fatal illnesses. It also leaves out human costs associated with the other 71 cents that are lost with each dollar of debt service (apart from the 29 cents in forgone public health expenditure) owing to reduced spending on education, infrastructure and other public goods.

In Chapter 3 we showed that for every dollar of foreign borrowing by African governments in the 1970–2008 period, roughly 60 cents left the country in the same year as capital flight. This means that four of the seven infant deaths associated with each million dollars of debt service can be attributed to loans that funded capital flight. Applying this ratio to the $19.2 billion annual debt service paid in 2005–07, we conclude that debt-fuelled capital flight resulted in 77,000 excess infant deaths per year.

These numbers give new meaning to the phrase 'blood money'. They illuminate the enormous human costs that Africa is suffering as a result of its financial haemorrhage, as public and private actors at home and abroad contrive to smuggle money overseas while mortgaging the continent's resources.

Asking African countries to mobilize more domestic resources and to use them better to improve the well-being of their people is only part of the development story. So is asking donors to provide more aid for investments in healthcare and other human needs in Africa. The other part of the story, equally if not more important, is the urgent need to find ways to keep Africa's resources onshore and to use them to improve the lives of the African people.

5 | The way forward

On 1 October 1898, peace commissioners appointed by the governments of the United States and Spain met in Paris, at a suite provided by the French Ministry of Foreign Affairs, to negotiate the terms for the end of the Spanish-American War. In the course of the war, which broke out in March of that year, the USA had wrested control of the erstwhile Spanish colonies of Cuba, the Philippines, Puerto Rico and Guam. The top item on the negotiators' agenda was responsibility for roughly $400 million in debts to foreign creditors owed by the Cuban government.[1]

The Spanish commissioners argued that repayment was the responsibility of Cuba's new government. The US commissioners, led by former Secretary of State William Day, rejected this claim, declaring that the debt 'had been imposed on the people of Cuba without their consent and by force of arms' and that 'the creditors, from the beginning, took the chances of the investment'.[2]

The US position prevailed. Under the terms of the Treaty of Paris, signed in December 1898, Cuba did not inherit responsibility for the liability, and the creditors were left to recoup whatever they could from the government of Spain.

Whether, and under what circumstances, governments are bound to honour debts contracted by their predecessors, even after a constitutional rupture in the continuity of the state, has been debated by jurists and philosophers since the time of Aristotle.[3]

The Dutch scholar Hugo Grotius, sometimes described as 'the father of international law', held in 1625 that contracts should not be honoured 'where public money has been pledged for purposes that are not for the public good'.[4]

Writing in 1927, the exiled Russian jurist Alexander Nahum Sack coined the modern term for such debts: *dettes odieuses*, or odious debts.[5]

Odious debt and international law

A nation's debts can be considered odious if three conditions hold:

1 *Absence of consent*: The debts were incurred without the consent of the people. This is typically the case when the debts were incurred by an undemocratic regime, such as a military dictatorship.

2 *Absence of benefit*: The borrowed funds were not used for the public benefit, but instead for the private benefit of the ruler and his associates. The absence-of-benefit condition is evidently met when loans are used in ways that actively harm the people, for example by financing state repression. But it is also met when loans are used to fund capital flight.

3 *Creditor awareness*: The creditors were aware – or should have been aware – of both of the above conditions.[6]

The principle that public debts are odious when contracted for the private benefit of rulers and their associates, rather than for the benefit of the public, was upheld in 1923 by US Supreme Court Justice (and former president) William Howard Taft, who served as the arbitrator for a debt dispute between the governments of Costa Rica and Great Britain. The Costa Rican government had been overthrown in 1917 by Federico Tinoco, who established a military dictatorship. Shortly before his regime collapsed and Tinoco fled the country in 1919, his government obtained loans from the Royal Bank of Canada. The proceeds were used personally by Tinoco and his brother. The new civilian government repudiated these debts. The British government, acting on behalf of the bank, claimed that Costa Rica's new government was bound to honour them.

Taft ruled in favour of the government of Costa Rica. In his decision he stated that the bank 'must make out its case of actual furnishing of money to the government for its legitimate use. It has not done so. The bank knew that this money was to be used by the retiring president, F. Tinoco, for his personal support after he had taken refuge in a foreign country.'[7]

In ruling that the bank 'must make out its case', Chief Justice Taft assigned the burden of proof to the lender. It was not up to the Costa Rican government to trace Tinoco's accounts and try to recover the looted funds. Instead it was up to the bank to show that its loans were put to legitimate use.

The doctrine of odious debt draws not only from precedents in international law, but also from domestic law in the United States and the United Kingdom, to whose jurisdictions dispute resolution is often assigned in loan agreements. Both nations' legal traditions uphold the principle of *domestic agency*, which states that 'the very power of making a binding commitment for another person carries with it the special responsibility of acting in the interest of that person'.[8]

When the agent (in this case, the government) makes a binding debt commitment in the name of the principal (the people), it has the obligation to do so in the latter's interest. When the agent fails to meet this obligation, the legitimacy of the principal's liability can be challenged under the law.

In addition, in Anglo-American domestic law 'a third party can be held liable for assisting an agent in the breach of his obligations toward his principal', as Ashfaq Khalfan and his colleagues observe in a study of the odious debt doctrine published by the Montreal-based Centre for International Sustainable Development Law. 'So if a bank were to knowingly assist an executive to defraud a corporation, that bank can be held liable for the losses of the principal.'[9] By the same logic, if a bank were to knowingly assist a government official in defrauding a sovereign state, the bank can be held liable for the losses of the country's people.[10]

Odious debt includes but is not limited to 'criminal debt', the term applied to money borrowed by governments that is 'stolen by government officials, their families, and associates'.[11] Such debt clearly meets the absence-of-consent and absence-of-benefit conditions for odious debt; and, at least in settings where such theft is commonplace, it meets the creditor awareness condition, too.

A second subset of odious debt is 'despotic debt', a term

6 The revolving door between foreign borrowing and capital flight has left the African people paying debt service on loans from which they did not benefit (Associated Press/Sayyid Azim)

that can be given to money borrowed by a government that is used to maintain the power of the regime and suppress popular discontent. In Chapter 1 we encountered the example of debts incurred to finance civil war in Congo-Brazzaville, leading to the travesty that 'now the survivors must pay for the arms that killed their loved ones'. Some of the debts contracted by South Africa's apartheid regime fall into the same category.[12]

The definition of odious debt rests explicitly on how the money was used, not on whether servicing the debt would impose hardship on the people of the borrowing country. The latter criterion is typically invoked in calls for 'debt relief' and 'debt forgiveness'. From this standpoint the actual uses to which the borrowed funds were put does not matter. From the standpoint of whether a debt can be designated as odious, however, the actual use of the borrowed money is crucial.

It is also worth noting that the definition of odious debt does not rest simply on a comparison between benefits and costs. Of course, the costs to the public of servicing odious debt exceed its benefits, since the latter are zero (or, in the case of despotic debt, less than zero). But costs can be greater than benefits for other reasons, too, such as inefficiency or ineptitude, as opposed to odious misuse of the funds. If, for example, a loan is used to finance an investment project that turns out to earn a rate of return below the interest rate on the loan, the resulting costs exceed the benefits. Such imprudent debts are *onerous* in that the public would have been better off without them, but they are not *odious* as the term is used in international law.

The debts of sovereign nation-states can thus be partitioned into distinct components, based upon where the borrowed money went. Figure 5.1 depicts the categories discussed above. At the broadest level, sovereign debt can be divided into onerous debt and virtuous debt, based on the loan's net benefit to the public. Where benefits exceed costs, the loan is virtuous; where costs exceed benefits, the loan is onerous.[13] 'Benefits' here may include consumption, as when loans are used to import food or medicine, as well as prudent investments. Onerous debt can be subdivided

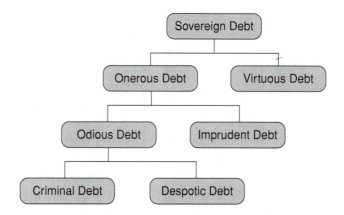

5.1 Types of sovereign debt

into odious debt and imprudent debt; and odious debt can be further subdivided into criminal debt and despotic debt.

It is not always easy to determine which specific debts fall into which category. Suppose, for example, that a $10 million loan was used to fund an unprofitable investment project. At first blush this may look like imprudent debt, onerous but not odious. But what if the investment's unprofitability is due to the fact that substandard materials were procured at inflated prices, so as to yield $1 million in kickbacks for government officials and another $1 million in profit to the politically connected businessmen who got the procurement contracts? What if the officials and business-men then moved their loot into offshore accounts – perhaps even in the same bank that provided the loan? Should the remaining $8 million that was squandered on the white elephant be regarded as merely imprudent debt, while the $2 million that was stolen and spirited abroad is odious? Or instead should the 'investment' be regarded as, in effect, merely a fat transaction cost for a project whose true purpose was to line private pockets, in which case the entire debt could be regarded as odious?

Answers to such questions may not be straightforward. Such complications are not unusual in legal disputes. Without them, the world would need far fewer lawyers. But the difficulties posed by blurred boundaries do not detract from the value and importance of distinguishing between odious debt and the other categories. The fact that it may be hard to determine whether a particular death was caused by murder does not mean that we should not have laws against homicide.

Looking at the different types of sovereign debt shown in Figure 5.1, it is natural to ask how much of Africa's debt falls into each category. The evidence presented in this book supports the conclusion that a substantial fraction of Africa's total debt can be regarded as criminal, and hence subject to treatment as odious debt under international law. If roughly 60 cents of every dollar of new borrowing spun out the revolving door as capital flight in the same year it was borrowed, this implies not only that much capital flight from sub-Saharan Africa was debt-fuelled, but also that more than half of African debt is odious.

Odious debts or odious governments?

Two broad strategies have been proposed for tackling the issue of odious debt. The first, drawing on precedents such as the Cuban debt and the Tinoco arbitration, is for governments to repudiate odious debt contracted by previous regimes. We call this the *ex post* strategy, since it deals with odious debt contracted in past years. The second strategy is to vest an international institution with the power to designate specific governments as odious, after which designation of any new debts contracted by that regime can be declared odious by successor governments. We call this the *ex ante* strategy, since it deals with debts to be contracted in the future by a government once it has been declared odious. The two strategies have quite different implications for African countries, as we explain below.

The ex post *strategy* Two main issues must be dealt with in order to establish the ground rules for implementing the *ex post* strategy. The first is assignment of the burden of proof: is it up to indebted governments to prove that debts they want to repudiate are odious, or must the creditors prove that debts whose legitimacy has been challenged are not odious? The second issue is determining the appropriate body for adjudication of odious-debt disputes. Clearly, neither the debtor nor the creditor qualifies as an impartial arbiter of the status of the debt. A neutral third party must perform this function. Who?

In many cases, placing the burden of proof upon the governments of indebted countries to establish the odious character of debts could impose an insuperable hurdle. The money trail by which borrowed funds left the country as capital flight was typically not carefully recorded.

When there are reasonable grounds to believe that widespread theft of borrowed funds took place under previous governments, an alternative approach is to place the burden of proof upon the creditors to demonstrate the legitimacy of debts contracted by those regimes. A recent article in the *Duke Law Journal* endorses this approach, citing US domestic law:

> We believe that governmental corruption in some countries is so suffocatingly ubiquitous that a U.S. court could legitimately shift onto the plaintiff [i.e. a creditor seeking redress for non-repayment] the burden of showing that a particular transaction was *not* tainted by corruption [...] Against a showing of pervasive corruption, is it unreasonable to ask the plaintiff/lender to explain how it alone had managed to preserve its virtue in dealing with the corrupt regime?[14]

Applying this legal strategy, sub-Saharan African governments could inform their creditors that outstanding debts will be treated as legitimate if, and only if, the real counterparts of the debts can be identified and shown to have benefited the people of the country, or at least shown to have had a reasonable prospect of benefiting them. If the creditors can document where the money went, and show that the loan was virtuous or at worst merely imprudent, then the debt would continue to be treated as a bona fide external obligation of the government. But if the fate of the borrowed money cannot be traced, then the arbiter can infer that the loan was diverted into the private pockets of individuals linked to the former regime. In such cases, the liability for the debt can be argued to lie not with the current government, but with those individuals whose personal fortunes are the real counterpart to the debt. If the creditors want to recover their money, they must seek redress from those individuals, not from the government.

This strategy would accord symmetric treatment to Africa's external assets and external liabilities. When African governments seek to reclaim stolen funds, such as money held in the Swiss bank accounts of corrupt ex-rulers, they must establish the legitimacy of their claims. By the same token, when creditors who lent money to those rulers seek to collect debt-service payments from the new government, they too can be required to establish the legitimacy of their claims.

The case for symmetry is reinforced by the complicity of the creditors in keeping corrupt rulers in power and helping them move their ill-gotten gains abroad. An editorial in London's *Financial Times* commented on the freezing of Swiss bank accounts of Nigerian dictator Sani Abacha: 'Financial institutions that knowingly channelled the funds have much to answer for, acting not so much as bankers but as bagmen, complicit in the corruption that has crippled Nigeria.'[15] As we have seen, Abacha was not an isolated case.

The second issue is who will adjudicate odious debt disputes between African governments and their creditors. If indebted countries could simply repudiate odious debt unilaterally, with no recourse to legal proceedings to assess the merits of the case, there is an evident risk that they would adopt an overly expansive definition of what constitutes an odious debt. To be sure, governments that abuse the odious debt doctrine would be likely to lose access to further credit, even for legitimate purposes, but this threat may not be a terribly strong deterrent for reasons explained below.

At the present time, the only bodies with legal authority to handle such disputes are courts in the political jurisdictions specified in loan documents. In most, if not all, cases, these courts are located in the creditor countries. If an African government seeks to repudiate odious debts, it must mount legal challenges in these foreign courts on a loan-by-loan basis, with the court then deciding if the loan is odious in whole or in part. This route would be costly, though perhaps not as costly as continuing to service odious debts.

Alternatively, the international community could establish a new institution specifically charged with the task of adjudicating disputes over debt legitimacy. In 2005 the Norwegian government called for the creation of an 'international debt settlement court' for just this purpose.[16] This proposal has much to recommend it, as it could not only ensure judicial independence but also reduce legal costs.

Would creditors retaliate against governments that challenge odious debts by refusing to lend to them in future years? This concern was raised after the 1986 downfall of the Marcos dictatorship in the Philippines, when Citibank president John Reed came to Manila and warned the new government of President Corazon Aquino that if it were to repudiate the Marcos debts, this 'would produce immense suffering and difficulty for the people'.[17]

Such threats may prove to be paper tigers for three reasons. First, invocation of the odious debt doctrine is not the same as across-the-board debt repudiation. Legitimate creditors have no reason to fear, since legitimate loans will be repaid. Secondly, for countries now experiencing negative net transfers – that is, paying more in debt service than they receive in new loans – the benefit of repudiation would exceed the cost of retaliation. Thirdly, those lenders who genuinely want to promote development – and we can hope that there are some, especially among the official creditors whose resources ultimately come from taxpayers of the industrialized countries – will have good reason to welcome steps to ensure that their money goes into productive investment rather than being used directly or indirectly to service odious debts. Indeed, aid donors who want to help clean up the legacy of odious debts could provide legal assistance for this purpose. Going a step farther, they could even make some aid conditional on steps to stem the squandering of scarce resources on odious debt service.

Proponents of the *ex ante* strategy described below have objected to the *ex post* strategy on the grounds that 'any adjudicating body that had the power to declare debt void might nullify legitimate debt if it placed a high value on the welfare of the debtor country', arguing that this could jeopardize future access to legitimate loans and thereby harm the country.[18] Such actions would be a rather perverse form of favouritism. But this concern again underscores the need for an impartial institution to adjudicate odious debt disputes.

The ex ante *strategy* In the *ex ante* strategy, an international referee – such as the IMF – would be charged with the task of determining not which debts are odious, but rather which governments are odious. Creditors who lend to a government that has been designated 'odious' would do so at their own risk. Successor governments not only can repudiate such loans, but in fact would be *required* to do so in order to prevent new loans from being wasted on odious debt service. Proponents argue that if the referee assesses government legitimacy truthfully, and if creditors act rationally, little or no odious debt will be forthcoming in the international financial marketplace. They also argue that this mechanism for disciplining odious regimes would be superior to conventional economic sanctions, because it would be less likely to affect adversely the population of the country.[19]

The *ex ante* approach has several weaknesses, however. First and foremost, it would leave untouched the burden of past debts, a large portion of which may deserve to be classified as odious. African countries therefore would remain snared in the debt trap left by irresponsible borrowing and complacent lending in the past. The strategy would let both parties – past corrupt governments and their financiers – off the hook at zero cost.

Secondly, it is no easy matter to entrust an international institution with the task of deciding which regimes are odious. Donor governments, the international financial institutions and even non-governmental organizations often have political interests in supporting existing regimes, or at least in refraining from alienating them. Influential governments could seek to veto rulings against client regimes, and press for unfavourable outcomes for disfavoured regimes. There may also be a bias against declaring the governments of economically powerful countries to be odious, whereas smaller countries, including most African nations, may be more likely to be penalized.

Thirdly, this strategy could perpetuate or exacerbate what economists call 'moral hazard' on both sides of the market. Regimes not designated as odious can continue to divert borrowed funds into private pockets, and creditors can happily turn a blind eye to these diversions, being assured that their loans cannot be labelled odious debts.

Finally, there may be some scope for legitimate lending even to odious governments, if and when the loans would benefit the people of the country. To ensure the legitimacy of such loans, creditors would have to exercise due diligence by monitoring uses of the money, and by suspending disbursements in cases of misuse. The *ex ante* designation of odious governments, by virtue of its all-or-nothing character, would deter such lending. In contrast, the *ex post* strategy leaves room to be selective.

These considerations lead us to conclude that the *ex post* strategy offers a superior way to address the problem of odious debt. The selective repudiation of odious debts would relieve the people of Africa of the burden of debt service on loans that fuelled capital flight. It would also have a salutary effect on incentive structures throughout the international financial system. The risk of repudiation of odious debts would give creditors a powerful motive to exercise due diligence, to demand transparency from borrower governments regarding the use of loans and to ensure that their loans do not fuel capital flight. The *ex post* strategy neither opens the financial tap for indiscriminate lending to some governments nor shuts it altogether to block all flows to others. Instead of a stark on-or-off choice, it would allow for flexibility to calibrate the quantity and quality of the flow of international credit.

Conclusions

During the past four decades sub-Saharan Africa has experienced a financial haemorrhage. We estimate that from the thirty-three countries for which we have data, capital flight between 1970 and 2008 amounted to $735 billion in 2008 dollars. Including imputed interest earnings, the drain of resources amounted to $944 billion. These sums far surpass the same countries' combined external debts, which stood at $177 billion in 2008. This means that sub-Saharan Africa is *a net creditor* to the rest of the world.

If this is true, why are so many of Africa's people so poor? The answer, of course, is that the subcontinent's external assets are private and in the hands of a narrow and wealthy stratum of its population, whereas its external debts are public and therefore borne by the people as a whole through their governments.

Foreign loans helped to fuel Africa's capital flight, as we have shown in this book. Indeed, some of the same banks that provided loans to African governments also provided international private banking services to wealthy Africans who stashed funds abroad. Our statistical estimates indicate that half or more of the money flowing into Africa as foreign loans exited in the same year as capital flight.

The negative economic impact of debt-fuelled capital flight on African economies is not immediate. Initially they experience both the inflow of borrowed money and the outflow of capital flight. If all the borrowed money were to exit immediately through the revolving door, the initial net effect would be zero; and if only part of the borrowed money fuels capital flight, the country receives a net inflow. The real drain on African economies comes later, when the country repays the debts that fuelled capital flight.

From 1970 to 2008, the thirty-three countries analysed in this book spent $490 billion (in 2008 dollars) on external debt service – principal repayments and interest payments on foreign loans. The outflow rose over time, swelling from less than $5 billion per year in the 1970s to more than $15 billion per year in 2000–08.[20]

The cost of Africa's debt service can be measured in human as well as financial terms. If these billions had been invested in health and education, millions of lives could have been saved. Millions more African children could have completed school. Of course, we cannot assume that all of the money spent on debt service would have otherwise been devoted to meeting the basic human needs of the population. In Chapter 4 we obtained a more conservative estimate of the human cost of debt service, by examining statistically the relationship between the percentage of GDP that African countries spend on debt service and the percentage that they spend on public health. We found that a billion dollars of annual debt service is associated with a reduction in annual public health expenditure of roughly $290 million. We estimated that this translates into about seven thousand additional infant deaths per year.

The revolving door between foreign loans and capital flight from Africa points to deep perversions in the incentive structure of international finance. On both the borrower and lender sides of international credit markets, there is a fateful disjuncture between the incentives facing the 'agents' who make decisions and the interests of the 'principals' whom they are supposed to represent. On the borrower side, rulers incur public debts in the name of their people, and then divert much of the money into their own pockets and those of their family relations, friends and associates. On the creditor side, loan officers are rewarded and promoted for 'moving the money', even as they load the balance sheets of the institutions that employ them with subprime assets that will prove difficult or impossible to recover.

The picture we have painted in this book is not a pretty one. Nor is it a picture that the agents who spin the revolving door are eager to see put on public display. But understanding these pathologies of international finance is the first step towards liberating Africa from the debt trap, freeing resources for human needs and economic development, and preventing further capital flight and financial misconduct in the future.

Solutions to the twin problems of capital flight and odious debts are possible. The necessary steps include:

97

- *Seek to recover stolen wealth*: Efforts by African governments to recover stolen assets have won modest international backing in the Stolen Asset Recovery (StAR) initiative launched in 2007 by the World Bank and the United Nations Office on Drugs and Crime. Much more could and should be done to chart Africa's money trail, identify looters and their accomplices, and repatriate the stolen funds. The amounts likely to be recovered by such efforts amount to a small fraction of Africa's total stolen wealth, but the proceeds can at least cover the costs of discovery and recovery. More important than the monetary return, however, is the light that such efforts can shine into the shadows of international finance, as illustrated by the cases we cited in our opening chapter. Greater public awareness will help build demand for initiatives to remedy the systemic weaknesses that are the root of the problem.

- *Curtail money laundering*: International banks have been active collaborators in efforts to move stolen assets abroad and hide them from public view. Curtailing these practices will require better enforcement of existing laws, passage of new legislation, and coordinated international efforts to curb financial flows to bank secrecy jurisdictions that refuse to take these actions.[21] With respect to enforcement, for example, although United States law on paper bars the entry of proceeds from theft by foreign government officials (as well as the proceeds of drug trafficking and bank fraud), Raymond Baker and Eva Joly, leading authorities on illicit financial flows, report that 'U.S. Treasury Department officials estimate that 99.9 percent of the money that U.S. law prohibits from entering the country is accepted for deposit the first time it is presented to a U.S. bank'.[22] The need for new legislation is illustrated by the fact that US law currently does not bar proceeds from handling stolen property, foreign tax evasion and numerous other activities carried out abroad that would be crimes if committed in the USA itself.[23]

- *Strengthen transparency*: Much can be done to make information on financial inflows to African governments more accessible to the African public, thereby making theft of the incoming funds more difficult. A good example of such an initiative is the Publish What You Pay campaign that was launched in 2002 by an international NGO coalition, which calls for corporations involved in natural resource extraction to disclose all payments to governments.[24] Along similar lines, a Publish What You Fund campaign, calling for timely disclosure of disbursements by aid donors, was launched at the OECD's High-Level Forum on Aid Effectiveness meeting in Accra in 2008. A similar initiative for private creditors – call it 'Publish What You Lend' – could usefully complement these campaigns. Steps to strengthen transparency can go hand in hand with efforts to deepen democracy – together these are the building blocks for financial accountability.

Repudiate odious debts: Finally, there is both an opportunity and the necessity to attack the nexus between foreign loans and capital flight by selectively repudiating those debts that are odious. Precedents for this can be found both in international law and in the domestic laws of creditor countries. Where there is ample evidence that debt-fuelled capital flight has been widespread, as in many African countries, the onus can be placed upon creditors to demonstrate that their loans were used for legitimate purposes. If the creditors cannot do so, African governments should politely but firmly refuse to service the resulting debts. In such cases, creditors should be encouraged to seek to recover the funds from the individuals who stole the money – some of which may be held in private accounts in the same banks. African countries can initiate such legal actions unilaterally. Their task can be facilitated by support from the international community in the forms of legal assistance and establishment of an international body to adjudicate debt disputes.

These measures will not only benefit the people of Africa. They will also improve the functioning of our international financial system, benefiting borrowers and lenders worldwide in years to come. The current practice of attempting to service all external debts, regardless of the uses to which the borrowed money in fact was put, is inefficient as well as unjust. Insured against the consequences of malfeasance, creditors lack incentives to minimize this risk. Greater transparency, coupled with the prospect of selective repudiation of odious debts, would strengthen their incentives to exercise due diligence. This would benefit African countries by curtailing debt-fuelled capital flight. It would also benefit the creditors themselves by reducing the need for debt reschedulings and write-offs in future years.

Steps to enforce and reward responsible lending practices by international creditors and to promote responsible and transparent debt management by African governments will yield win-win outcomes for all except those who currently profit by exploiting vulnerabilities in the international financial system. First and foremost, the people of Africa will benefit from measures to stop the bleeding of the continent through capital flight and odious debt service. The taxpayers of creditor countries will also benefit, as their money is no longer dissipated in poorly managed official loans and bailouts for private creditors. So, too, will the shareholders of private banks, who will earn honest returns on good loans rather than being saddled with bad loans from which they ultimately stand to recover only pennies on the dollar.

The people of Africa, the taxpayers of creditor countries and the shareholders of private banks share a common interest in overcoming the 'principal-agent' problems described in this book. They are the principals in whose name the agents – African rulers, officials of international financial institutions and government credit agencies, and loan officers of private banks – conduct the business of international finance. The fact that misconduct is rampant means that we must join together to enact reforms to ensure that the agents serve us rather than helping themselves to our money. In international finance, as in much of life, good principles are good for principals.

Appendix 1 Tables

TABLE A.1 External debt, 2008

Country	Billion US$	% of GDP
Angola	15.1	18
Botswana	0.4	3
Burkina Faso	1.7	21
Burundi	1.4	124
Cameroon	2.8	12
Cape Verde	0.6	36
Central African Republic	0.9	48
Chad	1.7	21
Congo, Dem. Rep.	12.2	105
Congo, Rep.	5.5	51
Côte d'Ivoire	12.6	54
Ethiopia	2.9	11
Gabon	2.4	16
Ghana	5.0	31
Guinea	3.1	72
Kenya	7.4	22
Lesotho	0.7	42
Madagascar	2.1	23
Malawi	1.0	23
Mauritania	2.0	69
Mozambique	3.4	35
Nigeria	11.2	5
Rwanda	0.7	15
São Tomé & Principe	0.2	102
Seychelles	1.5	181
Sierra Leone	0.4	20
South Africa	41.9	15
Sudan	19.6	34
Swaziland	0.4	14
Tanzania	5.9	29
Uganda	2.0	17
Zambia	3.0	21
Zimbabwe	5.2	186
TOTAL	176.9	19

Source: World Bank, World Development Indicators and Global Development Finance database

TABLE A.2 Capital flight by country

Country	Total real capital flight ($ million, in constant 2008 dollars)	Ratio of real capital flight to 2008 GDP (%)	Total capital flight stock with interest, 2008 ($ million)	Ratio of capital flight stock to debt (%)
Angola	71,513.0	85.8	79,962.3	528.5
Botswana	1,828.7	14.1	-204.5	-46.7
Burkina Faso	1,134.0	14.3	2,872.7	170.9
Burundi	4,464.3	383.9	5,065.2	350.6
Cameroon	24,042.1	102.8	33,256.4	1,190.1
Cape Verde	3,456.4	199.8	4,056.2	649.4
Central African Rep.	2,400.4	121.8	3,285.8	346.1
Chad	2,035.1	24.3	3,034.8	173.5
Congo, Dem. Rep.	30,725.1	265.1	48,441.5	397.1
Congo, Rep.	23,899.7	223.4	26,903.1	490.5
Côte d'Ivoire	45,454.3	194.1	66,247.1	527.4
Ethiopia	20,122.7	76.0	25,953.7	900.5
Gabon	18,159.6	125.8	21,854.1	923.4
Ghana	10,608.5	65.8	13,565.1	272.9
Guinea	917.3	21.5	1,430.5	46.3
Kenya	7,120.8	20.6	10,990.5	147.7
Lesotho	705.6	43.5	1,176.9	172.5

Madagascar	9,375.1	104.5	12,154.7	582.8
Malawi	2,292.8	53.7	3,695.7	383.7
Mauritania	3,607.4	126.2	5,399.2	275.5
Mozambique	14,520.2	149.2	18,442.0	537.3
Nigeria	296,220.8	139.7	376,855.2	3,358.6
Rwanda	4,417.8	99.1	7,009.4	1,031.9
São Tomé & Principe	1,073.1	614.6	1,428.1	803.2
Seychelles	4,104.5	492.7	4,527.7	300.8
Sierra Leone	6,092.1	311.9	8,725.7	2,244.3
South Africa	36,160.9	13.1	36,431.4	86.9
Sudan	18,739.3	32.1	25,699.3	130.9
Swaziland	2,088.0	79.8	2,255.4	622.5
Tanzania	6,713.8	32.8	11,354.4	191.2
Uganda	13,886.1	116.8	15,988.5	807.6
Zambia	24,411.9	170.5	35,051.9	1,173.7
Zimbabwe	22,623.0	807.6	31,338.3	602.8
TOTAL	734,914.2	80.8	944,246.0	533.6

Source: Authors' computations

TABLE A.3 Infant mortality, public health expenditure and debt service by country (annual average for 2005–07, measured in current US$)

Country	Infant mortality rate (per 1,000 live births)	Public health expenditure per capita	Public health expenditure as % of GDP	Debt service as % of GDP
Angola	133	52	2.0	8.6
Botswana	27	291	4.8	0.5
Burkina Faso	95	15	3.6	0.8
Burundi	103	6	4.7	4.4
Cameroon	85	12	1.2	3.4
Cape Verde	26	86	3.6	2.8
Central African Rep.	116	6	1.6	3.5
Chad	124	15	2.4	1.0
Congo, Dem. Rep.	126	2	1.2	4.1
Congo, Rep.	78	32	1.5	1.2
Côte d'Ivoire	84	8	0.9	1.9
Ethiopia	74	5	2.3	0.9
Gabon	59	217	3.1	9.0
Ghana	55	19	3.3	2.0
Guinea	95	2	0.7	5.2
Kenya	80	12	1.9	2.1
Lesotho	70	27	3.6	4.9

Madagascar	71	9	2.6	1.0
Malawi	73	11.5	5.1	2.1
Mauritania	75	13	1.6	3.9
Mozambique	98	12	3.7	0.8
Nigeria	99	17	1.8	4.4
Rwanda	80	15	4.7	0.9
São Tomé & Príncipe	64	48	5.9	6.5
Seychelles	11	411	3.8	12.4
Sierra Leone	130	4	1.6	1.5
South Africa	49	196	3.6	1.8
Sudan	70	13	1.4	1.1
Swaziland	64	104	4.4	1.4
Tanzania	72	12	3.1	0.7
Uganda	88	6	1.8	1.2
Zambia	96	30	3.8	2.2
Zimbabwe	63	11	4.2	3.5
SIMPLE AVERAGE	80	52	3.0	3.1
POPULATION-WEIGHTED AVERAGE	87	26	2.4	2.6

Note: Public health expenditure per capita and debt service/GDP for Zimbabwe are calculated as the annual average of 2003 to 2005 owing to lack of data. The figure for public health expenditure for Burundi is calculated using data from the Ministry of the Economy, Finance, and Development Cooperation as reported in the PRSP Report (IMF 2009).

Source: World Bank, World Development Indicators database

Appendix 2 Senior policy seminar on capital flight in sub-Saharan Africa

Summary outcome and policy recommendations (Pretoria, 3 November 2007)

The Association of African Central Bank Governors, the South African Reserve Bank, the African Development Bank, the African Capacity Building Foundation, the Bank of England, the Belgium Development Cooperation, the US Department of Treasury and the World Bank jointly organized a senior policy seminar on the implications of capital flight for macroeconomic management and growth in sub-Saharan Africa between 30 October and 3 November 2007. Other partner institutions included the University of Cape Town, the University of Ibadan, New York University, the Institute of Development Studies at Sussex, the University of Massachusetts at Amherst, the University of Birmingham and Venture Partners Botswana.

Hosted by the South African Reserve Bank, this seminar came at a time of renewed interest in increased domestic resources mobilization in support of investment and growth for poverty alleviation following the debt crisis, falling investments, assets decumulation and continued increase of capital flight.

Indeed, over the last four decades, capital flight – the voluntary exit of private residents' own capital for safe havens away from sub-Saharan Africa – has grown unabated, including during the highly indebted poor countries (HIPC) era. Recent estimates suggest that since 1970, capital flight from sub-Saharan Africa has increased continuously, reaching the dramatic threshold of half a trillion US dollars in 2004, more than twice the size of aggregate external liabilities of the region. And between 1999 and 2004 capital flight estimates from the region were about US$80 billion, with more than US$35 billion recorded in 2003, the largest single annual outflow over the decades following independence. An annual outflow of this magnitude suggests that capital flight indeed remains a serious problem and may undermine Africa's development and attainment of the Millennium Development Goals. The excess of capital flight from sub-Saharan Africa over its external liabilities does indeed suggest that the region is a 'net creditor to the rest of the world'.

While this financial haemorrhage draining domestic savings is not peculiar to sub-Saharan Africa, its costs for investment, growth and welfare to the region have been significant, and larger compared to other regions of the developing world. These costs have been further magnified by a marginalization of the region on the landscape of global capital flows, with the sub-Saharan African region accounting for less than 4 per cent of FDI flows to developing countries.

According to Professor Njuguna Ndung'u, the governor of the Central Bank of Kenya, who gave the keynote address at the opening of the seminar, 'capital flight has had adverse welfare and distributional consequences on the overwhelming majority of the poor in numerous countries in that it heightened income inequality and jeopardized employment prospects in sub-Saharan Africa'. Similarly, HE Jan Mutton, the ambassador of Belgium in South Africa, stressed 'the importance of good governance for growth and economic development', and reiterated 'the commitment of the Belgium government to promoting transparency at the international level'.

Opening this continental event, Professor Brian Kahn, the Deputy Chief Economist of the South African Reserve Bank, encouraged participants to the seminar to seek operational policies to stem and reverse capital flight, arguing that 'if domestic residents are exporting their capital why would foreign capital come in'. To mitigate the costs of this financial haemorrhage, the seminar brought together international experts and senior African policy-makers to discuss the implications of capital flight for macroeconomic management and growth in sub-Saharan Africa, and review policy options to stem and reverse capital flight and enhance growth in the region. The key recommendations that emerged from this seminar are outlined below.

Appendix 2

Policy recommendations The participants to the seminar invariably stressed the significant costs of capital flight for a long-run persistency under the debt-poverty trap in sub-Saharan Africa over the past decades. The delegates also recognized that increasing prospects for domestic resource mobilization are critical for investment and poverty reduction. In particular, the research presented during the seminar showed that the repatriation of 25 per cent of flight capital to source countries would increase investment rates to over 30 per cent of GDP in sub-Saharan Africa, the highest rate in the developing world. In this regard, the delegates called for the implementation of a number of key policy recommendations to stem and reverse the ongoing and consistently rising trend of capital flight. Key among this set of policy recommendations are the following:

1. *Improve the domestic investment environment*: In order to both prevent further capital flight and induce the repatriation of legitimately acquired capital now held abroad by Africans, it is crucial for African governments to implement measures to improve the environment for investment and the investment climate in Africa. A number of specific measures suggested include: (i) strengthening the rule of law, including the protection of property rights; (ii) public investment in infrastructure and 'human capital' that complements and 'crowds in' private investment; (iii) transparent, predictable and consistent taxation policies; and (iv) where appropriate, targeted tax amnesties for repatriated capital (as implemented by South Africa's government in 2003/04 with considerable success).

2. *Recovery of stolen assets*: In order both to recover illegitimately acquired capital that has flown abroad in search of a 'safe haven' and deter future loot-and-run behaviour, an all-out effort should be made to identify and recover stolen assets currently hidden in bank accounts and other investments overseas. A large portion of these assets is in liquid form and could be recovered with the cooperation of international banking institutions. The Stolen Asset Recovery (StAR) initiative launched in September by the World Bank and the United Nations Office of Drugs and

Crime (UNODC) reflects growing international recognition of the urgency of tackling this issue. International cooperation – measures by Western governments to deny safe havens to illicitly acquired wealth looted from Africa – is essential to the success of such initiatives. The recovery of assets should be coupled with the recovery of information about how assets have been looted, transferred, and hidden from the view of financial authorities and the public; in other words, StAR should go hand in hand with Stolen Asset Information Recovery (StAIR) – the information stairway to asset recovery.

3. *Challenge the legality of odious debts*: Statistical analysis reveals that approximately 60 cents of every dollar of external borrowing by Africa in the period 1970–2004 left the continent in the same year, a phenomenon that economists term 'debt-fuelled capital flight'. In other words, the creation of public external debts went hand in hand with the creation of private external assets. The legitimacy of debts that financed capital flight can be challenged under both international law and domestic law in creditor countries, including that of the United States and the United Kingdom, the countries to whose jurisdictions dispute resolution is often designated in loan agreements. In international law, odious debts are defined by three conditions: (i) they were incurred without the consent of the people; (ii) they did not benefit the people; and (iii) the creditors were aware (or should have been aware) of the absence of consent and absence of benefit. In domestic law, agents (in this case, African governments) who incur debts on behalf of principals (African peoples) have the obligation to act in the interest of the principals; liabilities to creditors who abet agents who breach this obligation are illegitimate. By challenging the legality of odious debts, African governments can both stem the haemor-rhage of scarce resources to service these debts and improve the operation of international financial markets in future years so as to encourage responsible lending and discourage irresponsible management of borrowed funds.

4. *Economic and financial intelligence:* In Western countries,

banks are required to report transactions exceeding a threshold level to government authorities (in the United States, for example, the threshold is $10,000). Such information should be shared with responsible authorities in the countries from which such transactions originate. The ability to track illicit financial movements has been strengthened in recent years as a result of efforts to curtail terrorism. These advances should be applied to efforts to curtail the flight of illicitly acquired funds from Africa and other developing countries. A number of sub-Saharan African countries are already working with the US Treasury and other bilateral donors to establish the Economic and Financial Intelligence Unit (FIU) to track financial flows and prevent illicit capital flight and money laundering. The delegates recommended expanding the coverage of FIU to include the majority of African countries.

5. *Proactive role for the Association of African Central Bank (AACB) Governors*: The delegates felt that the AACB Governors was the most appropriate body to play the lead role in advocating the implementation of these policy recommendations. In particular, they recommended that the AACB play a more proactive role in gathering and sharing information on capital flight, working closely with the OECD and representatives of the StAR initiative and bilateral donor countries, some of which constitute safe havens for capital flight. The delegates also recognized that strong support and cooperation at the international level were essential and could enhance the mandate of the AACB Governors. Additionally, they highlighted the critical role and expected benefits of sensitizing the global development community and African countries on the scale of financial haemorrhage caused by capital flight. A number of specific policy measures suggested in this regard include the following:

- improve information-sharing through the adoption of international rules;
- encourage and facilitate the ability of banks and other financial institutions to freely exchange information on tax and capital flight;

- involve African countries individually and as a group in international initiatives, to maximize information exchanges on their nationals' and companies' assets held abroad in offshore centres;
- promote the development of financial and capital markets to expand prospects for investment and portfolio diversification in sub-Saharan Africa, including through an increase in the scope of domestic investment of African sovereign capital, building on a stronger reserve position achieved over the last few years;
- avoid falling back to unsustainable external debt ratios, particularly by ensuring that external borrowings in the post-HIPC completion-point era are primarily used for the expansion of productive investment, with high economic returns and prospects for increasing economic diversification and export potential to mitigate exposure to terms-of-trade shocks;
- establish Financial Intelligence Units;
- improve the dissemination of information by statistical offices and compile quarterly flow-of-funds accounts to enable better multinational surveillance and disclosure;
- strengthen existing institutions, improve governance and the rule of laws to mitigate risks of corruption and capture of public assets by private agents;
- accelerate human resources development to expand the capacity to manage the repatriation of flight capital;
- develop efficient processes for payments and transfers of funds, including through the modernization of infrastructures and computerization of financial transactions;
- effect a proper sequencing of capital account liberalization;
- build strong regulatory institutions and framework in support of financial sector development;
- align the exchange rate to remove overvaluation, creating a conducive investment climate for local investors;
- mobilize support of key national, regional and international institutions to enhance the repatriation of flight capital and monitoring of returns;

- organize a follow-up conference either at a regional or global level focusing on repatriation of capital flight and economic growth in sub-Saharan Africa;
- organize follow-up seminars on estimation and monitoring of capital flight at the national level as part of institutional capacity-building;
- in addition the actions undertaken by the AACB Governors would be greatly enhanced if steps were taken by African governments to increase investments in strategic development projects that will have quick wins and promote other economic activities, provide incentives to enhance repatriation of flight capital, strengthen the role of the civil society in fostering accountability so that officials who are caught money laundering suffer the full cost of the law, and strengthening the functions of investigative journalism.

The international community has a role to play in this process of stemming and reversing flight capital. While capital flight involves actors in source and recipient countries, the burden of repatriation should be largely shouldered by the recipient countries. It is also important to:

- establish an international tribunal to arbitrate cases of corruption and capital flight;
- nullify banks' secrecy laws and policy of confidentiality, and hence pave the way towards the disclosing of stolen money and assets;
- enforce transparency in international banking operations;
- intensify anti-money laundering and launch an international campaign for capital flight repatriation;
- support the international efforts to fight against illicit financial flows from developed as well as developing countries.

Notes

Introduction

1 Claiborne (1989).

2 'Visit of Zaire's president – Mobutu Sese Seko – remarks made by President Reagan and President Mobutu after meeting on Dec. 9, 1986', *US Department of State Bulletin*, April 1987.

3 Pound (1990a).

4 Young (1978: 185).

5 Blumenthal (1982: 154–5).

6 Finch (1988). See also Askin (1993).

7 Brooke (1988b).

8 Pound (1990b).

9 Pound (1990a: A4).

10 George Bush, 'Remarks following discussions with President Mobutu, June 29, 1989', Archives of the American Presidency Project, University of California, Santa Barbara.

11 Boyce (1993: chs 1–2).

12 Mann and Rempel (1988).

13 Butterfield (1986).

14 Verzola et al. (1991).

15 Boyce (1990). See also Boyce (1993: chs 10–11).

16 Bello (2009).

17 Richburg (1991).

18 Statement of Herman J. Cohen, Assistant Secretary for African Affairs, *The Situation in Zaire: Hearing Before the Subcommittee on African Affairs of the Committee on Foreign Relations*, United States Senate, 6 November 1991.

19 US General Accounting Office (1999: 62).

20 Ndikumana and Emizet (2005).

21 No one counted the bodies. Based on a survey of mortality rates across DRC, including deaths caused by disease and malnutrition as well as by violence, the Internal Rescue Committee (IRC 2008) estimated that 5.4 million excess deaths occurred between August 1998 and April 2007. The Human Security Report Project (2009) maintains that the baseline mortality rate for DRC used by the IRC was too low, and that for this among other reasons its estimate of the excess mortality rate (the difference between measured mortality and baseline mortality) was too high. The latter report nevertheless acknowledges (p. 5) that the death toll in the DRC was 'huge'.

22 The seminar's summary outcome and policy recommendations are reproduced in Appendix 2.

23 Ndikumana and Boyce (2010a, 2011).

24 Pastor (1990: 7).

25 Henry (1986: 20).

Notes

1 Tales from the shadows

1 Winters (2004). See also Winters (2002: 111).

2 Berkman (2008: 29).

3 Ibid.: 70–1.

4 Ibid.: 112, 142.

5 Ibid.: 76–7.

6 UNODC and World Bank (2007: 11).

7 Quoted in Scher (2005: 3).

8 World Bank (2007: 230).

9 Okonjo-Iweala (2005).

10 Peryman (2005).

11 Mekay (2006).

12 Pedriel-Vassière (2009).

13 Ibid.: 87.

14 Global Witness (2004: 22) and Shaxson (2007: 111–12).

15 IMF, 'Report on the Republic of Congo', 2001, p. 39, quoted by Global Witness (2004: 21). The statistical annexe to this report is available on the IMF's website, but the report itself is not.

16 Loik Le Floch-Prigent, *Affaire Elf, affaire d'état* (Paris: Cherche Midi, 2001), p. 108; quoted by Shaxson (2007: 115).

17 Global Witness (2009a: 50).

18 See Polgreen (2007) and Jubilee Network USA (2008).

19 Gueye et al. (2007: 67).

20 Poverty data for 2005, as reported in the World Bank's *World Development Indicators.*

21 Nossiter (2009a).

22 Nossiter (2009b).

23 Global Witness (2009a: 45).

24 Associated Press (1999).

25 Global Witness (2009a: 46).

26 Howden (2009).

27 Reed (1987: 317).

28 Ibid.: 301; Brooke (1988a).

29 Swartzendruber (2003: 3).

30 Nossiter (2009b).

31 Ackworth (1993).

32 Africa Analysis (1999).

33 Brooke (1988a) and *Wall Street Journal*, 2 August 1977.

34 Quoted in Gerth (1999).

35 WHO (2010: 49, 51).

36 For more on loan pushing, see Darity and Horn (1988) and Deshpande (1999).

37 Quoted in Suzuki and Nanwani (2005: 186).

38 World Bank (1998: 118).

39 Ibid.: 23.

40 See, for example, Hook (1995).

41 Payer (1982: 38).

42 Gadanecz (2004).

43 Gwynne (1987: 107).

44 McDonald (1982: 38), quoted by Gwynne (1987: 107–8).

45 Gwynne (1987: 108).

46 Ibid.: 41–2.

47 Quoted in Zweig (1995: 705). Commenting on Wriston's defence of sovereign lending, his biographer Phillip Zweig remarks that 'Wriston heaped scorn on the Chicken Littles at every opportunity' (p. 729).

48 Interview with Dr Nouriel Roubini in the film *Inside Job*, released by Sony Pictures, September 2010.

49 Nakamoto and Wighton (2007).

50 Morgenson (2010).

51 Godfrey (2011: 33).

52 US Government Accountability Office (2008: 25).

53 Shaxson (2011: 7).

54 Lessard and Williamson

(1987: 83). In a similar vein, Walter (1987: 105) observed, 'If confidentiality has value, then asset holders engaging in capital flight should be willing to pay for it.'

55 O'Toole (2010: 47).

56 Baker (2005: 257).

57 The World Bank data from which these percentages are calculated do not provide details on the composition of short-term debt.

58 'This is not the way capitalism was supposed to work,' comments Morgenson (2010). 'Privatizing gains and socializing losses is deeply unfair, thoroughly un-American. But that is precisely what has characterized the aftermath of the credit craze.'

59 Quoted in Gerth (1999).

60 Net transfers reported in the World Bank's *World Development Indicators* and *Global Development Finance* database.

61 MacDonald (1989).

62 See, for example, Gunter (2002) and Canel (2009).

2 Measuring African capital flight

1 UNECA-AU (2010).

2 IMF World Economic Outlook database. Omitting South Africa, the region's total GDP was $720 billion.

3 See, for example, Chang and Cumby (1991) and Hermes and Lensink (1992).

4 For further details, see Boyce and Ndikumana (2001) and Ndikumana and Boyce (2010a).

5 For details on the components of the balance of payments, see IMF (1993), *Balance of Payments Manual*, Washington, DC: IMF.

6 See, for example, the contributions to the volume edited by Lessard and Williamson (1987).

7 If the exchange rates of the currencies in which the debt is denominated experience significant fluctuations, the year-to-year changes in the dollar value of the stock of outstanding debt can differ markedly from the actual net flows during the year. For example, for a country that holds UK pound-denominated debt, a depreciation of the pound reduces the dollar valuation of this portion of its debt stock. To avoid the resulting biases in our estimates of capital flight, we adjust the change in the long-term debt stock to account for fluctuations in the exchange rate of the dollar against other currencies, using GDF data on the currency composition of the debt. For details, see Ndikumana and Boyce (2010a).

8 Early discussions of trade misinvoicing can be found in Bhagwati (1964) and Gulati (1987).

9 Even if the net effect amount of trade misinvoicing was zero, there is reason to consider misinvoicing as an important mechanism of capital flight. In such a case, it simply means that capital flight through export under-invoicing and import over-invoicing is offset by capital outflows to finance the undeclared portion of imports. Foreign

exchange to finance the latter could have been moved abroad by other mechanisms, such as cash transfers and wire transfers (Boyce 1993).

10 See, for example, Ajayi (1997) and Ndikumana and Boyce (1998).

11 World Bank (2006: 92).

12 IFAD (2007).

13 We are grateful to Dr Manuel Orozco of the Inter-American Dialogue in Washington, DC, for providing us with the African remittance inflow estimates prepared for the IFAD study, disaggregated and cross-tabulated by sending countries.

14 The IFAD estimates include remittance inflows from all countries, including intra-African transfers, but the data on the number of migrants and their remittance behaviour appears to be less reliable for intra-African flows.

15 The latter method was proposed first by Pastor (1990).

16 For several countries in the group, the data that are necessary to measure capital flight are not available for early years in the 1970–2008 time period. For six of the countries the series starts after 1980, and for eight others the series are incomplete in the 1970s. If complete information were available, the total reported here would likely be higher.

17 Our estimate is also fairly close to that of Kar and Cartwright-Smith (2010: 10), who estimate the magnitude of capital flight from sub-Saharan Africa at $624 billion (without imputed interest earnings) from 1970 to 2008. Kar and Cartwright-Smith (ibid.: 16) also compute a broader measure of 'illicit financial flows' that does not subtract foreign exchange used to finance unrecorded imports; this yields estimates that are roughly twice as high.

18 Ashman et al. (2010).

19 Shinn (2008).

20 Githinji and Adesida (2011: Table 1).

21 Recurrent shocks constitute an important threat to the welfare of the poor, especially in rural agricultural African communities. Evidence suggests that nearly 50 per cent of household poverty in Africa is caused by shocks, and that the effects of shocks last a long time (Dercon 2004; Bigsten and Shimeles 2008, 2011).

22 See African Development Bank and World Bank (2011).

23 Shinn (2008).

24 Merrill Lynch, Capgemini Ernst & Young (2009: 3–4).

25 Collier et al. (2001: 59, Table 1).

26 Merrill Lynch, Capgemini Ernst & Young (2009: 16).

27 Mafusire et al. (2010).

28 'Africa Infrastructure Country Diagnostic' 2009, published jointly by the World Bank, the African Development Bank, the African Union, Agence Française de Développement, the European Union, the New Economic Partnership for Africa's Development, the Public-Private

Infrastructure Advisory Facility, and the UK Department for International Development.

29 Government of Sierra Leone, 'Infrastructure development proposal', 2007.

30 Early in 2010 the commune received temporary relief following a visit by the country's president, who expressed shock that such a situation could have gone unnoticed for so long. On his instructions, the road was repaired.

31 MDG Africa Steering Group (2008).

32 UNECA (1999).

33 Fofack and Ndikumana (2010).

34 For discussion, see AfDB, OECD and UNECA (2010).

35 In Rwanda, for example, reforms in the tax system including the establishment of an autonomous tax revenue authority helped to increase domestic revenue from 8.4 per cent of GDP in 1993 to 14.2 per cent in 2008 (AfDB 2010: 22).

36 AfDB, OECD and UNECA (2010); Ndikumana and Abderrahim (2010).

37 Collier (2010).

38 AfDB (2010).

3 The revolving door

1 Naylor (1987: 21–2).

2 For the statistically minded, the correlation coefficient is approximately 0.6.

3 Ndikumana and Boyce (2003, 2011). We report similar results in Ndikumana and Boyce (2010b).

4 These bank deposit data are reported by the Bank for International Settlements at www.bis.org/statistics/bankstats.htm, Table 6B.

5 An attraction of this proxy measure is that unlike estimates of total capital flight it does not rely on debt data for its construction. This rules out any possibility of a spurious correlation arising from debt measurement errors.

6 See, for example, Collier et al. (2001).

7 Ndikumana and Boyce (2003).

8 Pastor (1990: 7).

9 Khan and Haque (1985) and Cuddington (1986).

10 Alesina and Tabellini (1989).

11 Total official development assistance to Africa declined from $38.9 billion in 1990 to $22.5 billion in 2000 (in constant 2008 dollars), rising thereafter to $39.1 billion in 2008, of which $35.7 billion went to sub-Saharan Africa (data from World Bank, World Development Indicators database).

12 Collier et al. (2004).

13 Ndikumana and Boyce (1998). See Quazi (2004) for a case study on Bangladesh.

14 World Bank (2003: 10); Global Witness (2002: 4).

15 Where oil-backed loans are readily available, the leverage of the official creditor institutions to push for reforms of any type is quite limited. 'The IMF is holding out carrots,' explained one observer, while 'industry is holding out T-bone steaks' (quoted by Hoyos and Reed 2003).

16 Global Witness (1999: 15–18).

17 Shaxson (2001). For example, when it assembled a $455 million oil-backed loan to Angola in March 2001, Standard Chartered Bank reportedly had a 'huge oversubscription' from eager creditors.

18 BBC (2002). See also Cauvin (2002).

19 Global Witness (2002: 22).

20 The empirical analysis of the relationship between capital flight and natural resource revenues is made difficult by incomplete data on the latter. In earlier investigations we were able to find a positive relationship between oil exports and capital flight, but the relationship was not robust to econometric specifications that included country-specific 'fixed effects' (Ndikumana and Boyce 2011). For the purposes of this book, we revisited this relationship using our updated time series on capital flight and more complete data on oil exports, drawn from the African Development Bank's database. Using these data, the positive relationship remains statistically significant even in the fixed-effects specification.

21 See Ndikumana and Abderrahim (2010).

22 Brautigam (2010).

23 Osei and Mubiru (2010).

24 Brautigam (2009, 2010).

25 Guillaumont and Guillaumont-Jeanneney (2009).

26 'Kinshasa's missing millions', *Africa-Asia Confidential*, 3(4), February 2010.

27 Brautigam (2010).

28 Pallister (2005).

29 Ghazvinian (2007: ch. 7).

30 Ndikumana (2010).

31 This is, of course, not an easy matter. For more on international assistance and state-building, see Boyce and O'Donnell (2007); Boyce and Forman (2010).

4 The human costs

1 Pedriel-Vassière (2009: 88).

2 AfDB, UNECA, AU, UNDP (2010: 29).

3 WHO (2010).

4 AfDB (2009).

5 Coghlan et al. (2006).

6 Rolling Back Malaria (n.d.). Also see AfDB, UNECA, AU, UNDP (2010).

7 Rolling Back Malaria (2010).

8 Sachs (2005: 199).

9 Ibid.: 200. International funding for malaria has increased significantly in recent years (from $0.3 billion in 2003 to nearly $1.7 billion in 2009), but it still falls far short of the 2010 target of $6 billion (Rolling Back Malaria 2010).

10 WHO (2010: 64, 69).

11 Global Witness (2009b).

12 Global Witness (2011). A spokesperson for the government of Equatorial Guinea stated that the German-designed yacht was never ordered to be built, but that if it had been Obiang 'would have bought it with income from his private business activities' (Smith

2011). For an account of his business activities, see Silverstein (2011).

13 Global Witness (2009a).

14 WHO (2010: 38).

15 Ibid.: 124.

16 Ibid.: 144–8.

17 UNICEF (2002: 11).

18 Black et al. (2003).

19 World Bank and IMF (2010: 18).

20 See, among others, Anand and Ravallion (1993) and Cutler et al. (2006).

21 Cutler and Miller (2005).

22 MDG Africa Steering Group (2008).

23 The data are from the African Development Bank database.

24 The regression of infant mortality on public health expenditure per capita, both in logarithms, yields a coefficient of –0.26. This implies that a 1 per cent increase in spending is associated with a 0.26 per cent reduction in infant mortality. The calculations reported in the text are based on total public health expenditures for sub-Saharan Africa of \$22.6 billion and total infant deaths of 2.2 million infant deaths in 2007.

25 This relationship also holds when we control for differences in per capita income.

26 One Foundation (2010: 16).

5 The way forward

1 Musicant (1998: 607). The Cuban debt of \$400 million in 1898 would be equivalent to roughly \$10 billion in today's dollars.

2 Quoted in Adams (1991: 164).

3 In his Politics, Aristotle asked 'whether it is right or wrong for a state to repudiate public obligations when it changes its constitution to another form'. Quoted in Buchheit et al. (2007: 1206).

4 Howse (2007: 8).

5 Sack (1927).

6 For discussions on the definition of odious debt, see Sack (1927), Hoeflich (1982), Khalfan et al. (2003), King (2007) and Howse (2007). See also Luddington et al. (2010), who argue on the basis of a close reading of domestic law that the first condition (absence of consent, or a dictatorial regime) is not required for a finding of odious debt.

7 Quoted in Buchheit et al. (2007: 1217).

8 Khalfan et al. (2003: 3).

9 Ibid.: 3.

10 For discussion of this point, see Jochnick (2006) and Buchheit et al. (2007).

11 Winters (2002: 107).

12 Walker and Nattrass (2002).

13 Buchheit et al. (2007: 1211) define virtuous debt somewhat differently to mean borrowing that 'will benefit the people expected to repay the debt, even if that benefit is temporally remote'. This definition does not explicitly consider the magnitude of benefits relative to the costs of borrowing; our definition makes this weighing of relative costs and benefits explicit,

without specifying precisely how benefits are to be translated into monetary present values.

14 Ibid.: 1252.

15 Financial Times (2000).

16 See the Soria Moria Declaration on International Policy, October 2005; available at www.dna.no/index.gan?id=47619&subid=0.

17 Quoted in Boyce (1993: 332).

18 Jayachandran and Kremer (2006: 83).

19 Kremer and Jayachandran (2002, 2003).

20 See Figure 1.4.

21 For more on the topic of bank secrecy jurisdictions, see Shaxson (2011) and the excellent websites of the Tax Justice Network and Global Financial Integrity.

22 Baker and Joly (2009: 62–3).

23 Examples of the latter activities include counterfeiting, credit fraud, tax evasion and environmental crimes.

24 For an assessment, see van Oranje and Parham (2009).

Bibliography

Achebe, C. (2000) *Home and Exile*, New York: Anchor Books.

Ackworth, W. (1993) 'Oil keeps Gabon a hot paper, though debt remains unpaid', *LDC Debt Report*, 6(20): 5, 24 May.

Adams, P. (1991) *Odious Debts: Loose Lending, Corruption, and the Third World's Environmental Legacy*, London: Earthscan.

AfDB (African Development Bank) (2009) *African Development Report 2008/09. Conflict Resolution, Peace and Reconstruction in Africa*, London: Oxford University Press.

— (2010) *Domestic Resource Mobilization for Poverty Reduction in East Africa: The Case of Rwanda*, Tunis.

AfDB and World Bank (2011) *Leveraging Migration for Africa: Remittances, Skills and Investment*, Washington, DC: World Bank and AfDB.

AfDB, OECD and UNECA (United Nations Economic Commission for Africa) (2010) *African Economic Outlook 2010*, Paris and Tunis.

AfDB, UNECA, AU, UNDP (2010) *MDG Report 2010. Assessing Progress in Africa toward the Millennium Development Goals*.

Africa Analysis (1999) 'Gabon seeks way out of payment crunch', *Financial Times Information, Global News Wire*, 5 February.

Africa-Asia Confidential (2010) 'Kinshasa's missing millions', 3(4), February.

Ajayi, I. S. (1997) 'An analysis of external debt and capital flight in the severely indebted low income countries in sub-Saharan Africa', IMF Working Paper WP/97/68.

Alesina, A. and G. Tabellini (1989) 'External debt, capital flight and political risk', *Journal of International Economics*, 27: 199–220.

Anand, S. and M. Ravallion (1993) 'Human development in poor countries: on the role of private incomes and public services', *Journal of Economic Perspectives*, 7(1): 133–50.

Ashman, S., S. Mohamed and S. Newman (2010) 'Preliminary Draft Submission of Comments in Response to the Proposals of Exchange Control Voluntary Disclosure Program and Amendment to the Exchange Rate Controls' (proposals by the South African Reserve Bank). University of Witwatersrand, Corporate Strategy and Industrial Development Research Programme (CSID), August.

Askin, S. (1993) 'Zaire: Part II: Accounting for Mobutu's sins: a government of theft', *EM Report*, 13 May.

Associated Press (1999) 'Some details on Citibank cases', *Associated Press Online*, 9 November.

Baker, R. (2005) *Capitalism's Achilles Heel: Dirty Money and How to Renew the Free-Market System*, New York: John Wiley & Sons.

Baker, R. and E. Joly (2009) 'Illicit money: can it be stopped?', *New York Review of Books*, 3 December, pp. 61–3.

BBC (2002) 'IMF: Angola's missing millions', 18 October.

Bello, W. (2009) 'Cory and the creditors', *Philippine Daily Inquirer*, 12 August.

Berkman, S. (2008) *The World Bank and the Gods of Lending*, Sterling, VA: Kumarian Press.

Bhagwati, J. N. (1964) 'On the underinvoicing of imports', *Bulletin of the Oxford University Institute of Statistics*, November.

Bigsten, A. and A. Shimeles (2008) 'Poverty transition and persistence in Ethiopia', *World Development*, 36(9): 1559–84.

— (2011) 'The persistence of urban poverty in Ethiopia: a tale of two measurements', *Applied Economics Letters*, 18(9): 835–9.

Black, R. E., S. S. Morris and J. Bryce (2003) 'Where and why are 10 million children dying every year?', *The Lancet*, 361, 28 June.

Blumenthal, E. M. (1982) 'Zaire: rapport sur la crédibilité financière internationale', in E. Dungia, *Mobutu et l'argent du Zaire: les révélations d'un diplomate ex-agent des services secrets*, annexe 2, Paris: L'Harmattan, pp. 136–55.

Boyce, J. K. (1990) *The Political Economy of External Indebtedness: A Case Study of the Philippines*, Monograph Series no. 12, Manila: Philippine Institute of Development Studies.

— (1992) 'The revolving door? External debt and capital flight: a Philippine case study', *World Development*, 20(3): 335–49.

— (1993) *The Philippines: The Political Economy of Growth and Impoverishment in the Marcos Era*, London: Macmillan, for the OECD Development Centre.

Boyce, J. K. and S. Forman (2010) 'Financing peace: international and national resources for postconflict countries and fragile states', Background paper for the *World Development Report 2011*, October.

Boyce, J. K. and L. Ndikumana (2001) 'Is Africa a net creditor? New estimates of capital flight from severely indebted sub-Saharan African countries, 1970–1996', *Journal of Development Studies*, 38(2): 27–56.

— (2005) 'Africa's debt: who owes whom?', in G. A. Epstein (ed.), *Capital Flight and Capital Controls in Developing Countries*, Northampton and Aldershot: Edward Elgar, pp. 334–40.

Boyce, J. K. and M. O'Donnell (eds) (2007) *Peace and the Public Purse: Economic Policies for Postwar Statebuilding*, Boulder, CO: Lynne Rienner.

Brautigam, D. (2009) *The Dragon's Gift: The Real Story of China in Africa*, Oxford: Oxford University Press.

— (2010) 'Africa's eastern promise: what the West can learn from Chinese investment in Africa', *Foreign Affairs*, online feature article, 5 January.

Brooke, J. (1988a) 'African railroad running a deficit', *New York Times*, 23 May, p. D10.

— (1988b) 'Mobutu's village basks in his glory', *New York Times*, 29 September.

Buchheit, L. C., G. Mitu Gulati and R. B. Thompson (2007) 'The dilemma of odious debts', *Duke Law Journal*, 56: 1201–62.

Butterfield, F. (1986) 'Filipinos say Marcos was given millions for '76 nuclear contract', *New York Times*, 7 March, pp. A1, A9.

Canel, J. (2009) 'Debt relief but at what cost?', *Stanford Journal of International Relations*, 11(1): 6–15.

Cauvin, H. E. (2002) 'I.M.F. skewers corruption in Angola', *New York Times*, 30 November, p. A6.

Chang, K. P. H. and R. E. Cumby (1991) 'Capital flight in sub-Saharan African countries', in I. Husain and J. Underwood (eds), *African External Finance in the 1990s*, Washington, DC: World Bank, pp. 162–87.

Claiborne, W. (1989) 'Mobutu refurbishing image tainted by corruption charge', *Washington Post*, 29 June, p. A27.

Coghlan, B., R. J. Brennan, P. Gnoy, D. Dofara, B. Otto, M. Clements and T. Stewart (2006) 'Mortality in the Democratic Republic of Congo: a nationwide survey', *The Lancet*, 367: 44–51.

Collier, P. (2010) 'In Afghanistan, a threat of plunder', *New York Times*, 19 July.

Collier, P., A. Hoeffler and C. Pattillo (2001) 'Flight capital as a portfolio choice', *World Bank Economic Review*, 15(1): 55–80.

— (2004) 'Aid and capital flight', Oxford: Centre for the Study of African Economies.

Cuddington, J. (1986) 'Capital flight: estimates, issues, and explanations', *Princeton Studies in International Finance*, 58, Princeton University, Department of Economics.

Cutler, D. M. and G. Miller (2005) 'The role of public health improvements in health advances: the twentieth-century United States', *Demography*, 42(1): 1–22.

Cutler, D. M., A. S. Deaton and A. Lleras-Muney (2006) 'The determinants of mortality', Working Paper 1193, Cambridge, MA: National Bureau of Economic Research, January.

Darity, W., Jr, and B. Horn (1988) *The Loan Pushers: The Role of the Commercial Banks in the*

International Debt Crisis, Cambridge, MA: Ballinger.

Dercon, S. (2004) 'Shocks and growth: evidence from rural Ethiopia', *Journal of Development Economics*, 74: 309–29.

Deshpande, A. (1999) 'Loan pushing and triadic relations', *Southern Economic Journal*, 65(4): 914–26.

Financial Times (2000) 'Nigeria seeks help in tracing billions taken by former military leaders', 23 July, p. 5.

Finch, D. (1988) 'Let the IMF be the IMF', *International Economy*, January/February, pp. 126–8.

Fofack, H. and L. Ndikumana (2010) 'Capital flight repatriation: investigation of its potential gains for sub-Saharan african countries', *African Development Review*, 22(1): 4–22.

Gadanecz, B. (2004) 'The syndicated loan market: structure, development and implications', *BIS Quarterly Review*, December, pp. 75–89.

Gbesemete, K. P. and U. G. Gerdtham (1992) 'Determinants of health care expenditure in Africa: a cross-sectional study', *World Development*, 20(2): 303–8.

Gerth, J. (1999) 'Hearings offer view into private banking', *New York Times*, 8 November.

Ghazvinian, J. (2007) *Untapped: The Scramble for Africa's Oil*, Orlando, FL: Harcourt.

Githinji, M. wa and O. Adesida (2011) *Industrialization, Exports and the Developmental State in Africa*, Uppsala: Nordic Africa Institute, forthcoming.

Global Witness (1999) *A Crude Awakening: The Role of the Oil and Banking Industries in Angola's Civil War and the Plunder of State Assets*, London, December.

— (2002) *All the Presidents' Men*, London, March.

— (2004) *Time for Transparency: Coming Clean on Oil, Mining and Gas Revenues*, London, March.

— (2009a) *Undue Diligence: How Banks Do Business with Corrupt Regimes*, London, March.

— (2009b) *The Secret Life of a Shopaholic. How an African dictator's playboy son went on a multi-million-dollar shopping spree in the U.S.*, London: Global Witness.

— (2011) 'Son of Equatorial Guinea's dictator plans one of world's most expensive yachts', Press release, 28 February.

Godfrey, A. B. (2011) 'Of elusive corruption and slippery panacea: towards understanding corruption under the NRM in Uganda', Paper presented at the Conference on Corruption and the Pursuit of Accountability in Africa, Mt Holyoke College, South Hadley, MA, 27/28 February.

Gueye, C. F., M. Vaugeois, M. Martin and A. Johnson (2007) 'Negotiating debt reduction in the HIPC Initiative and beyond',

Publication no. 11, London: Debt Relief International.

Guillaumont, P. and S. Guillaumont-Jeanneney (2009) 'Accounting for vulnerability of African countries in performance-based aid allocation', Working Paper no. 103, African Development Bank.

Gulati, S. K. (1987) 'A note on trade misinvoicing', in D. R. Lessard and J. Williamson (eds), *Capital Flight and Third World Debt*, Washington, DC: Institute for International Economics, pp. 68–78.

Gunter, B. G. (2002) 'What's wrong with the HIPC Initiative and what's next?', *Development Policy Review*, 20(1): 5–24.

Gupta, S., M. Verhoogen and E. Tiongson (2001) 'Public spending on health and the poor', IMF Working Paper WP/01/127, Washington, DC: International Monetary Fund.

Gwynne, S. C. (1987) *Selling Money*, New York: Penguin Books.

Henry, J. (1986) 'Where the money went: Third World debt hoax', *New Republic*, 14 April, pp. 20–3.

Hermes, N. and R. Lensink (1992) 'The magnitude and determinants of capital flight: the case for six sub-Saharan African countries', *The Economist*, 140(4): 515–30.

Hoeflich, M. E. (1982) 'Through a glass darkly: reflections upon the history of the international law of public debt in connec-tion with state succession', *University of Illinois Law Review*, 1: 39–70.

Hook, S. W. (1995) *National Interest and Foreign Aid*, Boulder, CO: Lynne Rienner.

Howden, D. (2009) 'The corrupt nepotist who ruled Gabon for 40 years', *Independent* (London), 9 June.

Howse, R. (2007) 'The concept of odious debt in public international law', Discussion Paper no. 185, Geneva: United Nations Conference on Trade and Development (UNCTAD).

Hoyos, C. and J. Reed (2003) 'Angola forced to come clean', *Financial Times*, 2 October, p. 14.

Human Security Report Project (2009) 'The shrinking costs of war', Burnaby, BC: Simon Fraser University.

IFAD (International Fund for Agricultural Development) (2007) *Sending Money Home: Worldwide Remittance Flows to Developing and Transition Countries*, Rome: IFAD, www.ifad.org/events/remittances/maps/brochure.pdf.

IMF (1993) *Balance of Payments Manual*, Washington, DC: IMF.

— (2005) *Country Report on Angola No. 05/228*, July.

— (2009) *Country Report on Angola No. 09/320*, November.

— (2010) *World Economic Outlook* database, October.

IRC (International Rescue Committee) (2008) 'Mortality in the Democratic Republic of

Congo: an ongoing crisis', Washington, DC: IRC.

Jayachandran, S. and M. Kremer (2006) 'Odious debt', *American Economic Review*, 96(1): 82–92.

Jochnick, C. (2006) 'The legal case for debt repudiation,' in C. Jochnick and F. A. Preston (eds), *Sovereign Debt at the Crossroads*, Oxford: Oxford University Press, pp. 132–57.

Jubilee Network USA (2008) 'Vulture funds and poor country debt: recent developments and policy responses', Briefing Note no. 4, Washington, DC, April.

Kar, D. and D. Cartwright-Smith (2010) 'Illicit financial flows from Africa: hidden resource for development', Washington, DC: Global Financial Integrity.

Khalfan, A., J. King and B. Thomas (2003) *Advancing the Odious Debt Doctrine*, Working paper, Montreal: Centre for International Sustainable Development Law, 11 March.

Khan, M. and N. U. Haque (1985) 'Foreign borrowing and capital flight', *IMF Staff Papers*, 32: 606–28.

King, J. A. (2007) 'Odious debt: the terms of the debate', *North Carolina Journal of International Law and Commercial Regulation*, 32: 605–68.

Kremer, M. and S. Jayachandran (2002) 'Odious debt', Working Paper no. 8953, Cambridge, MA: National Bureau of Economic Research.

— (2003) 'Odious debt: when dictators borrow, who repays the loan?', *Brookings Review*, 21(2).

Lessard, D. R. and J. Williamson (eds) (1987) *Capital Flight and Third World Debt*, Washington, DC: Institute for International Economics.

Luddington, S., M. Gulati and A. L. Brophy (2010) 'Applied legal history: demystifying the doctrine of odious debts', *Theoretical Inquiries in Law*, 11: 247–81.

MacDonald, S. (1989) 'French woo Africa with debt write-off', *The Times* (London), 26 May.

McDonald, R. P. (1982) *International Syndicated Loans*, London: Euromoney Publications.

Mafusire, A., J. Anyanwu, Z. Brixiova and M. Mubila (2010) 'Infrastructure deficit and opportunities in Africa', *AfDB Economic Brief*, 1(2), 7 September.

Mann, J. and W. C. Rempel (1988) 'Marcos bids $5 billion to go home: offer for return to Philippines said to bar prosecution', *Los Angeles Times*, 26 July.

MDG Africa Steering Group (2008) *Achieving the Millennium Development Goals in Africa*, New York: United Nations.

Mekay, E. (2006) 'U.S. lawmakers call Nigerian debt "odious"', Inter Press Service News Agency, 7 January.

Merrill Lynch, Capgemini Ernst & Young (2002) *World Wealth Report 2002*.

— (2009) *World Wealth Report 2009*.

Morgenson, G. (2010) 'After the deluge: a look at Washington, Wall Street and Main Street post-meltdown', Philip Gamble Memorial Lecture, Department of Economics, University of Massachusetts, Amherst, 14 October.

Musicant, I. (1998) *Empire by Default: The Spanish-American War and the Dawn of the American Century*, New York: Henry Holt.

Nakamoto, M. and D. Wighton (2007) 'Citigroup chief stays bullish on buy-outs', *Financial Times*, 9 July.

Naylor, R. T. (1987) *Hot Money and the Politics of Debt*, New York: Simon and Schuster.

Ndikumana, L. (2010) 'Chine-Afrique: les projecteurs à nouveau braqués sur le continent', *African Business*, 12: 36–7.

Ndikumana, L. and K. Abderrahim (2010) 'Revenue mobilization in African countries: does natural resource endowment matter?', *African Development Review*, 22(3): 351–65.

Ndikumana, L. and J. K. Boyce (1998) 'Congo's odious debt: external borrowing and capital flight in Zaire', *Development and Change*, 29(2): 195–217.

— (2003) 'Public debts and private assets: explaining capital flight from sub-Saharan African countries', *World Development*, 31(1): 107–30.

— (2010a) 'Measurement of capital flight: methodology and results for sub-Saharan African countries', *African Development Review*, 22(4): 471–81.

— (2010b) 'Africa's revolving door: external borrowing and capital flight in sub-Saharan Africa,' in V. Padayachee (ed.), *The Political Economy of Africa*, London and New York: Routledge.

— (2011) 'Capital flight from sub-Saharan African countries: linkages with external borrowing and policy options', *International Review of Applied Economics*, 25(2): 149–70.

Ndikumana, L. and K. Emizet (2005) 'The economics of civil war: the case of the Democratic Republic of Congo', in N. Sambanis et al. (eds), *Understanding Civil War: Evidence and Analysis*, Washington, DC: World Bank.

Ndikumana, L. and J. Nannyonjo (2007) 'Uganda: from failed state to success story?', in J. K. Boyce and M. O'Donnell (eds), *Peace and the Public Purse: Economic Policies for Postwar Statebuilding*, Boulder, CO: Lynne Rienner.

Nossiter, A. (2009a) 'Omar Bongo, Gabon leader, dies at 73', *New York Times*, 9 June.

— (2009b) 'Libreville journal: underneath palatial skin, corruption rules Gabon', *New York Times*, 15 September.

Okonjo-Iweala, N. (2005) 'One in five Africans live in Nigeria

– and need aid', *Guardian* (London), 31 January.

One Foundation (2010) *The DATA Report 2010: Monitoring the G8 Promise to Africa*, London.

Organisation for Economic Cooperation and Development (OECD) and African Development Bank (AfDB) (2007) *African Economic Outlook 2007*, Paris: OECD.

Osei, B. and A. Mubiru (2010) 'Chinese trade and investment activities in Africa', *African Development Bank Policy Brief*, 1(4), 29 July.

O'Toole, F. (2010) *Ship of Fools: How Stupidity and Corruption Sank the Celtic Tiger*, New York: Public Affairs.

Pallister, D. (2005) 'Alarm bells sound over massive loans bankrolling oil-rich, graft-tainted Angola', *Guardian*, 1 June.

Pastor, M. (1990) 'Capital flight from Latin America', *World Development*, 18(1): 1–13.

Payer, C. (1982) *The World Bank: A Critical Analysis*, New York: Monthly Review Press.

Pedriel-Vassière, M. (2009) 'Oil-backed loans in Congo Brazzaville: potential legal remedies using the odious debt concept in the French legal system', in M. Mader and A. Rothenbuhler (eds), *How to Challenge Illegitimate Debt: Theory and Legal Case Studies*, Basle: AktionFinanzplatz-Schweiz, pp. 87–92.

Peryman, L. (2005) 'Debt cancellation sets looters free', *Odious Debts Online*, 24 October.

Polgreen, L. (2007) 'Unlikely ally against Congo Republic graft', *New York Times*, 10 December.

Pound, E. T. (1990a) 'Zaire's Mobutu mounts all-out PR campaign to keep his U.S. aid', *Wall Street Journal*, 7 March, pp. A1, A4.

— (1990b) 'IMF, World Bank aid has dealings hinting at conflict of interest', *Wall Street Journal*, 28 December, pp. A1–A2.

Quazi, R. (2004) 'Foreign aid and capital flight', *Journal of the Asia Pacific Economy*, 9(3): 370–93.

Reed, M. C. (1987) 'Gabon: a neo-colonial enclave of enduring French interest', *Journal of Modern African Studies*, 25(2): 283–320.

Richburg, K. (1991) 'Looting on the grand scale', *Guardian Weekly*, 13 October.

Rolling Back Malaria (2010) *World Malaria Day 2010: Africa Update*, Progress and Impact Series no. 2, April.

— (n.d.) Online information.

Sachs, J. (2005) *The End of Poverty: Economic Possibilities for Our Time*, New York: Penguin Press.

Sack, A. N. (1927) *Les Effets des transformations des états sur leurs dettes publiques et autres obligations financières*, Paris: RecueilSirey.

Scher, D. (2005) 'Asset recovery: repatriating Africa's looted billions', *Africa Security Review*, 14(4).

Shaxson, N. (2001) 'Angola secures loan from foreign banks', *Financial Times*, 23 March, p. 12.

— (2007) *Poisoned Wells: The Dirty Politics of African Oil*, New York: Palgrave Macmillan.

— (2011) *Treasure Islands: Tax Havens and the Men Who Stole the World*, London: Bodley Head.

Shinn, D. (2008) 'African migration and the brain drain', Paper presented at the Institute for African Studies and Slovenia Global Action, Ljubljana, June.

Silverstein, K. (2011) 'Teodorin's world', *Foreign Policy*, March/April.

SIPRI (2010) *SIPRI Yearbook 2010: Armaments, Disarmament and International Security*, Solna, Sweden: SIPRI.

Smith, D. (2011) 'Dictator's son had plans drawn up for £234m superyacht', *Guardian*, 28 February.

Suzuki, E. and S. Nanwani (2005) 'Responsibility of international organizations: the accountability mechanisms of multilateral development banks', *Michigan Journal of International Law*, 27: 177–225.

Swartzendruber, F. (2003) 'Trees, mines and pipelines: natural resource dependence and political instability in the Congo Basin', Kinshasa: Central African Research Programme for the Environment (CARPE), August.

Transparency International (2010) *Corruption Perceptions Index 2010.*

UNECA (1999) *Economic Report on Africa: The Challenges of Poverty Reduction and Sustainability*, Addis Ababa.

UNECA-AU (2010) ECA-AU Joint Press Release no. 26/2010, Lilongwe, Malawi, 29 March.

UNICEF (2002) *Finance Development – Invest in Children*, New York: UNICEF.

UNODC (United Nations Office on Drugs and Crime) and World Bank (2007) *Stolen Asset Recovery (StAR) Initiative: Challenges, Opportunities, and Action Plan*, Washington, DC: World Bank, June.

US General Accounting Office (1999) *International Monetary Fund: Observations on the IMF's Financial Operations*, Report GAO/NSAID/AIMD-99-252, September.

Us Government Accountability Office (2008) *International Taxation: Large U.S. Corporations and Federal Contractors with Subsidiaries in Jurisdictions Listed as Tax Haven or Financial Privacy Jurisdictions*, Report GAO-09-157, December.

Van Oranje, M. and H. Parham (2009) *Publishing What We Learned: An Assessment of the Publish What You Pay Coalition*, London: Publish What You Pay.

Verzola, R., M. Buenaventura and E. Santoalla (1991) 'The Philippine nuclear power plant: plunder on a large scale', in

A. Mendoza, Jr (ed.), *Debts of Dishonor*, vol. 1, Quezon City: Philippine Rural Reconstruction Movement, pp. 3–126.

Wagstaff, A. (2000) 'Socioeconomic inequalities in child mortality: comparisons across nine developing countries', *Bulletin of the World Health Organization*, 78(1): 19–29.

Walker, R. and N. Nattrass (2002) 'A critical analysis of the Jubilee 2000 (SA) call for cancelling South African government debt', *Development Southern Africa*, 19(4): 467–81.

Walter, I. (1987) 'The mechanisms of capital flight', in D. R. Lessard and J. Williamson (eds), *Capital Flight and Third World Debt*, Washington, DC: Institute for International Economics, pp. 103–28.

WHO (World Health Organization) (2010) *World Health Statistics*, Geneva: WHO.

Winters, J. A. (2002) 'Criminal debt', in J. R. Pincus and J. A. Winters (eds), *Reinventing the World Bank*, Ithaca, NY: Cornell University Press, pp. 101–30.

— (2004) 'Criminal debt', Testimony submitted to the United States Senate Committee on Foreign Relations, Hearing on 'Combating Corruption in Multilateral Development Banks', 13 May.

World Bank (various years), *Africa Development Indicators*.

— (1985) *World Development Report 1985*, Washington, DC: World Bank.

— (1998) *Assessing Aid: What Works, What Doesn't and Why*, New York: Oxford University Press.

— (2003) *Transitional Support Strategy for the Republic of Angola*, 4 March.

— (2006) *Global Economic Prospects 2006: Economic Implications of Remittances and Migration*, Washington, DC: World Bank.

— (2007) *Nigeria: A Fiscal Agenda for Change. Public Expenditure Management and Financial Accountability Review (PEMFAR)*, vol. 1: Main Report, 25 May.

World Bank and IMF (2010) *Global Monitoring Report 2010: The MDGs after the Crisis*, Washington, DC: World Bank and IMF.

Young, C. (1978) 'Zaire: the unending crisis', *Foreign Affairs*, 57: 169–85.

Zweig, P. L. (1995) *Wriston: Walter Wriston, Citibank, and the Rise and Fall of American Financial Supremacy*, New York: Crown Publishers.

Index

Henry, James, 10
high net worth individuals (HNWI), 47, 54
highly indebted poor countries (HIPC), 106
Hoeffler, Anke, 67

India, loans to Africa, 70–1
infant mortality *see* mortality, of infants
Inter-American Development Bank, 24
interest rates, 17, 25; negative, 30
International Fund for Agricultural Development (IFAD), 43–4
International Monetary Fund (IMF), 2–4, 8, 16, 17, 23, 33, 39, 54, 68, 75; *Direction of Trade Statistics*, 41
International Review of Applied Economics, 64
investment, 66; in Africa, improving environment of, 108; in infrastructure, 69; need for, 55–7
invoicing: misinvoicing, 40–2, 60 (as conduit for capital flight, 49–52); over-invoicing, 40, 50; under-invoicing, 40, 42, 49
Ireland, debt crisis in, 30

Joly, Eva, 98

Kahn, Brian, 107
Kenya: bond issue, 73; emigration of skilled professionals from, 53; remittance discrepancies in, 52
Khalfan, Ashfaq, 86
kleptocracy, 8
Kloberg III, Edward van, 4

Lansky, Meyer, 62
loan origination fees, 25
loan pushing, 23, 27
London Interbank Offered Rate (Libor), 25, 68

malaria, 71, 82; deaths from, 74, 75, 76
malnutrition, 78
Marcos, Ferdinand, 5, 93
McDonald, Robert P., 25
McKinsey & Company, 10
Merrill Lynch Global Wealth Management, 47
Millennium Development Goals (MDG), 56, 107; Africa Steering Group, 79; Global Monitoring Report, 78
Mitterrand, François, 37
Mobutu, Joseph, 1–5, 8, 12
money laundering, 62, 98, 110; combating of, 98, 112
moral hazard, 95
Morgenson, Gretchen, 27
mortality: from disease, preventable, 82; of children, 74, 76–8, 79; of infants, 82–3
mosquito nets, 74; distribution of, 71, 82
Mutton, Jan, 107

National Electric Power Authority (NEPA) (Nigeria), 14
Ndikumana, Léonce, 4–5, 8, 55–6; education of, 72
Ndung'u, Njuguna, 107
near-barter trade arrangements, 70
negative net transfers from Africa, 36, 93
Nigeria, 77, 92; capital flight from, 49; corruption of loan management in, 13–16; external debt of, 34; mis-invoicing in,

About Zed Books

Zed Books is a critical and dynamic publisher, committed to increasing awareness of important international issues and to promoting diversity, alternative voices and progressive social change. We publish on politics, development, gender, the environment and economics for a global audience of students, academics, activists and general readers. Run as a co-operative, Zed Books aims to operate in an ethical and environmentally sustainable way.

Find out more at:

www.zedbooks.co.uk

For up-to-date news, articles, reviews and events information visit:

http://zed-books.blogspot.com

To subscribe to the monthly Zed Books e-newsletter, send an email headed 'subscribe' to:

marketing@zedbooks.net

We can also be found on **Facebook**, **ZNet**, **Twitter** and **Library Thing**.